2020 Edit

Model Code of
UDICIAL CONDUCT

AMERICANBARASSOCIATION

Center for Professional
Responsibility

Cover design by ABA Design

The materials contained herein represent the opinions and views of the authors and/or the editors, and should not be construed to be the views or opinions of the law firms or companies with whom such persons are in partnership with, associated with, or employed by, nor of the American Bar Association unless adopted pursuant to the bylaws of the Association.

Nothing contained in this book is to be considered as the rendering of legal advice for specific cases, and readers are responsible for obtaining such advice from their own legal counsel. This book and any forms and agreements herein are intended for educational and informational purposes only.

Printed in the United States of America.

24 23 22 21   5 4 3 2

ISBN: 978-1-64105-673-1
e-ISBN: 978-1-64105-674-8

Discounts are available for books ordered in bulk. Special consideration is given to state bars, CLE programs, and other bar-related organizations. Inquire at Book Publishing, ABA Publishing, American Bar Association, 321 North Clark Street, Chicago, Illinois 60654.

www.ShopABA.org

ABA JOINT COMMISSION TO EVALUATE THE MODEL CODE OF JUDICIAL CONDUCT (2003-2007)

Mark I. Harrison
Phoenix, AZ, *Chair*

James J. Alfini
Houston, TX

Loretta C. Argrett
Washington, DC

Jan Witold Baran
Washington, DC

Dianne Cleaver
Kansas City, MO

Thomas M. Fitzpatrick
Tukwila, WA

Donald B. Hilliker
Chicago, IL

Hon. M. Margaret McKeown
San Diego, CA

Hon. Cara Lee T. Neville
Minneapolis, MN

Hon. Harriet L. Turney
Phoenix, AZ

Hon. James A. Wynn
Raleigh, NC

Reporters

Charles G. Geyh
Bloomington, IN

W. William Hodes
Indianapolis, IN

Advisors

Hon. Carol Bagley Amon
Judicial Conference of the United States

Hon. Peter W. Bowie
Judicial Conference of the United States

Robert P. Cummins
American Judicature Society

Marvin L. Karp
Standing Committee on Ethics and Professional Responsibility

M. Peter Moser
1990 Model Code Revision Project

D. Dudley Oldham
Standing Committee on Judicial Independence

Hon. Ellen F. Rosenblum
National Judicial College

Seth Rosner
Center for Professional Responsibility Coordinating Council

Chief Justice Randall T. Shepard
Conference of Chief Justices

Robert H. Tembeckjian
Association of Judicial Disciplinary Counsel

CONTENTS

Canon 3 33
A JUDGE SHALL CONDUCT THE JUDGE'S PERSONAL AND EXTRAJUDICIAL
ACTIVITIES TO MINIMIZE THE RISK OF CONFLICT WITH THE OBLIGATIONS OF
JUDICIAL OFFICE.

Rule

CONTENTS

PREFACE

In 1924, the American Bar Association adopted the Canons of Judicial Ethics that, according to Chief Justice William Howard Taft, who chaired the ABA Committee on Judicial Ethics, were intended to be a "guide and reminder to the judiciary."[1] The 1924 Canons of Judicial Ethics consisted of 36 provisions that included both generalized, hortatory admonitions and specific rules of proscribed conduct. The 1924 Canons were not intended to be a basis for disciplinary action. Many states, however, adopted this "guide" as a set of substantive rules, giving the Canons in those states the force of law with the added persuasion of sanctions for violations.[2]

Answering criticism that the 1924 Canons engaged in "moral posturing" that was more "hortatory than helpful in providing firm guidance for the solution of difficult questions,"[3] the ABA appointed a Special Committee on Standards of Judicial Conduct in 1969 to develop new ethics rules for judges. California Supreme Court Justice Roger J. Traynor chaired the Special Committee. After three years of work by the Special Committee, the Code of Judicial Conduct was adopted by unanimous vote of the ABA House of Delegates on August 16, 1972.[4] The 1972 Code was designed to be enforceable and was intended to preserve the integrity and independence of the judiciary.[5]

In 1986, the American Bar Association Standing Committee on Ethics and Professional Responsibility, with jurisdiction over the Code, conducted a survey that led to the conclusion that, in general, the Code was serving its purposes well, but that a comprehensive review of the Code was desirable. That review was conducted from 1987 to 1990 by the Standing Committee on Ethics and Professional Responsibility and its

---

1. *See* Randall T. Shepard, *Campaign Speech: Restraint and Liberty in Judicial Ethics*, 9 Geo. J. Legal Ethics 1059, 1065 n. 26 (1996) (citing the *Final Report and Proposed Canons of Judicial Ethics*, 9 A.B.A.J. 449, 449 (1923)).

2. *Id.* (citing Robert Martineau, *Enforcement of the Code of Judicial Conduct*, 1972 Utah L. Rev. 410, 410).

3. Robert McKay, *Judges, the Code of Judicial Conduct, and Nonjudicial Activities*, 1972 Utah L. Rev. 391, 391.

4. American Bar Association, *Report of the Special Committee on Standards of Judicial Conduct*, 96 Rep. of the A.B.A. 733-34 (1971).

5. *See* E. Wayne Thode, Reporter's Notes to the Code of Judicial Conduct (1973).

Judicial Code Subcommittee composed of several members and former members of the Ethics Committee and several members of the judiciary. This national effort was funded by the Josephson Institute for the Advancement of Ethics, the State Justice Institute, and the American Bar Association.

In the revision process, the Association sought and considered the views of members of the judiciary, the bar and the general public. The Committee was aware that the 1972 Canons, apart from their subsections, were used widely as a basis for discipline. Therefore, the Committee declined to replace the black letter language with descriptive headings and determined that the Code, consisting of statements of norms denominated Canons, specific Sections, and explanatory Commentary, stated the appropriate ethical obligations of judges.[6]

On August 7, 1990, the House of Delegates of the American Bar Association adopted the Model Code of Judicial Conduct. In the 1990 Code, a Preamble and a Terminology section were added, and an Application section followed the Canons. The 1990 Code was amended three times: on August 6, 1997; August 10, 1999; and August 12, 2003.

In September 2003, with a grant from The Joyce Foundation of Chicago, Illinois, the American Bar Association announced the appointment of the Joint Commission to Evaluate the Model Code of Judicial Conduct under the auspices of the ABA Standing Committee on Ethics and Professional Responsibility and the ABA Standing Committee on Judicial Independence. The mandate of the Commission was to review the 1990 Code and to recommend revisions for possible adoption. The eleven-member Commission was composed of judges, experts in the field of judicial and legal ethics and a public member and was supported by two reporters, ten advisors and counsel from the American Bar Association.

Over the course of three and one half years, the Commission conducted a comprehensive examination of the standards for the ethical conduct of judges and judicial candidates that promote the independence, integrity and impartiality of the judiciary. This examination was prompted, in part, by the collective experience of judges and judicial regulators who had worked with the 1990 Code for more than a decade and by the emergence of new types of courts and courts processes, the increasing frequency of pro se representation, and the utilization of di-

---

6. *See* LISA L. MILORD, THE DEVELOPMENT OF THE ABA JUDICIAL CODE at 8 (1992).

verse methods in the judicial selection process. This national effort culminated in the adoption of the revised Model Code of Judicial Conduct by the ABA House of Delegates on February 12, 2007.

The 2007 Code proposed both format and substantive changes to the 1990 Code. Following a format similar to the ABA Model Rules of Professional Conduct, the 2007 Code preserved the Canons, which state overarching principles of judicial conduct, followed by enforceable black letter Rules, and Comments that provide both aspirational statements and guidance in interpreting and applying the Rules. The four Canons and their numbered Rules and Comments were reorganized to provide topics under a functional arrangement. Canon 1 addresses the paramount obligations of judges to uphold the independence, integrity and impartiality of the judiciary and to avoid impropriety and its appearance; Canon 2 addresses solely the judge's professional duties as a judge; Canon 3 addresses extrajudicial and personal conduct; and Canon 4 addresses the political conduct of judges and judicial candidates. Also included are four sections that precede the Canons: a Preamble, which states the objectives of the Model Code; a new Scope section, which describes the manner in which the Canons and their Rules and Comments are to be interpreted, used for guidance, and enforced; a Terminology section, which provides definitional guidance, and an Application section, which establishes when the various Rules apply to a judge or judicial candidate.

This publication presents several informative appendixes that are not part of the Code. Appendix A contains Correlation Tables to the ABA Model Code of Judicial Conduct that compare the provisions of the 2007 Code with those of the predecessor 1990 Code. Appendix B reproduces the August 2010 Report to the House of Delegates that amended the Application section of the Code. Appendix C provides information on establishing judicial ethics advisory committees. Appendix D explains the jurisdiction and procedures of the ABA Standing Committee on Ethics and Professional Responsibility. Appendix E contains the most recent ABA judicial ethics opinions. A separate publication, the *Reporter's Notes to the Model Code of Judicial Conduct,* by Charles G. Geyh and W. William Hodes, provides detailed information regarding the drafting of the 2007 Code.

The American Bar Association continues to pursue its goal of assuring the highest standards of professional competence and ethical conduct. The Standing Committee on Ethics and Professional Responsibility, charged with interpreting the professional standards of the Association and recommending appropriate amendments and clarifications, issues opinions interpreting the Model Rules of Professional Conduct and the Model Code of Judicial Conduct. The opinions of the Committee are published by the American Bar Association.

JOINT COMMISSION TO EVALUATE THE MODEL CODE OF JUDICIAL CONDUCT
CHAIR'S INTRODUCTION

On September 23, 2003, American Bar Association President Dennis W. Archer, Jr., announced the appointment of a Joint Commission to Evaluate the Model Code of Judicial Conduct under the auspices of the Standing Committee on Ethics and Professional Responsibility and the Standing Committee on Judicial Independence. The last Model Code revision occurred in 1990 and, although specific provisions of the Model Code were amended in the intervening years, there was a need for a comprehensive evaluation and revision in light of societal changes, as well as changes in the role of judges. The Model Code revision project was funded almost entirely by the Joyce Foundation, which provides resources for countlessprojects that contribute to the betterment of our society.

The unanimous approval of the revised Model Code of Judicial Conduct by the ABA House of Delegates on February 12, 2007 culminated a three and one-half year effort by a group comprised of distinguished judges, lawyers, academicians and a public member. The work of the Joint Commission was significantly enhanced by the active participation of an advisory group comprised of representatives of the organizations principally involved in the work of the judiciary and in the enforcement of the rules governing judicial conduct, and the invaluable assistance of two able Reporters and Center for Professional Responsibility counsel and professional staff.

The revised Model Code is the product of a transparent process during which the Joint Commission held nine public hearings, met in-person twenty times, had more than thirty teleconferences, and regularly posted its work on its website with requests for feedback and comment. Although the Commission set out to preserve as much of the 1990 Code as it could, consistent with the process of overall evaluation, it carefully considered all submitted suggestions and criticism and incorporated many of the suggested changes into the revised Model Code that was adopted by the House of Delegates.

At the time of its adoption, the revised Model Code had the support of the Conference of Chief Justices and the co-sponsorship of the Judicial Division of the ABA, the ABA Standing Committees on Ethics and Professional Responsibility; Professional Discipline and on Judicial Independence, the ABA Sections of Litigation and Dispute Resolution, and the American Judicature Society. In light of this significant support from the judiciary and the profession, the Joint Commission expects that the highest court in each state will adopt the revised Model Code, thereby improving and clarifying the standards of conduct for the judiciary throughout the nation and creating national uniformity.

An independent, impartial judiciary is indispensable to our system of justice. Equally important is the confidence of the public in the independence, integrity and impartiality of our judiciary as an institution. In fulfilling its mission, the Joint Commission took great care to adhere to those principles as it worked to provide sound, clear, and reasoned guidance to judges faced with difficult issues involving their conduct. The end result is a Model Code that should serve both judges and the public well for many years to come.

Mark I. Harrison
April 2007

Preamble

[1] An independent, fair and impartial judiciary is indispensable to our system of justice. The United States legal system is based upon the principle that an independent, impartial, and competent judiciary, composed of men and women of integrity, will interpret and apply the law that governs our society. Thus, the judiciary plays a central role in preserving the principles of justice and the rule of law. Inherent in all the Rules contained in this Code are the precepts that judges, individually and collectively, must respect and honor the judicial office as a public trust and strive to maintain and enhance confidence in the legal system.

[2] Judges should maintain the dignity of judicial office at all times, and avoid both impropriety and the appearance of impropriety in their professional and personal lives. They should aspire at all times to conduct that ensures the greatest possible public confidence in their independence, impartiality, integrity, and competence.

[3] The Model Code of Judicial Conduct establishes standards for the ethical conduct of judges and judicial candidates. It is not intended as an exhaustive guide for the conduct of judges and judicial candidates, who are governed in their judicial and personal conduct by general ethical standards as well as by the Code. The Code is intended, however, to provide guidance and assist judges in maintaining the highest standards of judicial and personal conduct, and to provide a basis for regulating their conduct through disciplinary agencies.

Scope

[1] The Model Code of Judicial Conduct consists of four Canons, numbered Rules under each Canon, and Comments that generally follow and explain each Rule. Scope and Terminology sections provide additional guidance in interpreting and applying the Code. An Application section establishes when the various Rules apply to a judge or judicial candidate.

[2] The Canons state overarching principles of judicial ethics that all judges must observe. Although a judge may be disciplined only for violating a Rule, the Canons provide important guidance in interpreting the Rules. Where a Rule contains a permissive term, such as "may" or "should," the conduct being addressed is committed to the personal and professional discretion of the judge or candidate in question, and no disciplinary action should be taken for action or inaction within the bounds of such discretion.

[3] The Comments that accompany the Rules serve two functions. First, they provide guidance regarding the purpose, meaning, and proper application of the Rules. They contain explanatory material and, in some instances, provide examples of permitted or prohibited conduct. Comments neither add to nor subtract from the binding obligations set forth in the Rules. Therefore, when a Comment contains the term "must," it does not mean that the Comment itself is binding or enforceable; it signifies that the Rule in question, properly understood, is obligatory as to the conduct at issue.

[4] Second, the Comments identify aspirational goals for judges. To implement fully the principles of this Code as articulated in the Canons, judges should strive to exceed the standards of conduct established by the Rules, holding themselves to the highest ethical standards and seeking to achieve those aspirational goals, thereby enhancing the dignity of the judicial office.

[5] The Rules of the Model Code of Judicial Conduct are rules of reason that should be applied consistent with constitutional requirements, statutes, other court rules, and decisional law, and with due regard for all relevant circumstances. The Rules should not be interpreted to impinge upon the essential independence of judges in making judicial decisions.

[6] Although the black letter of the Rules is binding and enforceable, it is not contemplated that every transgression will result in the imposition of discipline. Whether discipline should be imposed should be determined through a reasonable and reasoned application of the Rules, and should depend upon factors such as the seriousness of the transgression, the facts and circumstances that existed at the time of the transgression, the extent of any pattern of improper activity, whether there have been previous violations, and the effect of the improper activity upon the judicial system or others.

[7] The Code is not designed or intended as a basis for civil or criminal liability. Neither is it intended to be the basis for litigants to seek collateral remedies against each other or to obtain tactical advantages in proceedings before a court.

Terminology

The first time any term listed below is used in a Rule in its defined sense, it is followed by an asterisk (*).

"Aggregate," in relation to contributions for a candidate, means not only contributions in cash or in kind made directly to a candidate's campaign committee, but also all contributions made indirectly with the understanding that they will be used to support the election of a candidate or to oppose the election of the candidate's opponent. See Rules 2.11 and 4.4.

"Appropriate authority" means the authority having responsibility for initiation of disciplinary process in connection with the violation to be reported. See Rules 2.14 and 2.15.

"Contribution" means both financial and in-kind contributions, such as goods, professional or volunteer services, advertising, and other types of assistance, which, if obtained by the recipient otherwise, would require a financial expenditure. See Rules 2.11, 2.13, 3.7, 4.1, and 4.4.

"De minimis," in the context of interests pertaining to disqualification of a judge, means an insignificant interest that could not raise a reasonable question regarding the judge's impartiality. See Rule 2.11.

"Domestic partner" means a person with whom another person maintains a household and an intimate relationship, other than a person to whom he or she is legally married. See Rules 2.11, 2.13, 3.13, and 3.14.

"Economic interest" means ownership of more than a de minimis legal or equitable interest. Except for situations in which the judge participates in the management of such a legal or equitable interest, or the interest could be substantially affected by the outcome of a proceeding before a judge, it does not include:

(1) an interest in the individual holdings within a mutual or common investment fund;

(2) an interest in securities held by an educational, religious, charitable, fraternal, or civic organization in which the judge or the judge's spouse, domestic partner, parent, or child serves as a director, an officer, an advisor, or other participant;

5

(3) a deposit in a financial institution or deposits or proprietary interests the judge may maintain as a member of a mutual savings association or credit union, or similar proprietary interests; or

(4) an interest in the issuer of government securities held by the judge.

See Rules 1.3 and 2.11.

"Fiduciary" includes relationships such as executor, administrator, trustee, or guardian. See Rules 2.11, 3.2, and 3.8.

"Impartial," "impartiality," and **"impartially"** mean absence of bias or prejudice in favor of, or against, particular parties or classes of parties, as well as maintenance of an open mind in considering issues that may come before a judge. See Canons 1, 2, and 4, and Rules 1.2, 2.2, 2.10, 2.11, 2.13, 3.1, 3.12, 3.13, 4.1, and 4.2.

"Impending matter" is a matter that is imminent or expected to occur in the near future. See Rules 2.9, 2.10, 3.13, and 4.1.

"Impropriety" includes conduct that violates the law, court rules, or provisions of this Code, and conduct that undermines a judge's independence, integrity, or impartiality. See Canon 1 and Rule 1.2.

"Independence" means a judge's freedom from influence or controls other than those established by law. See Canons 1 and 4, and Rules 1.2, 3.1, 3.12, 3.13, and 4.2.

"Integrity" means probity, fairness, honesty, uprightness, and soundness of character. See Canons 1 and 4 and Rules 1.2, 3.1, 3.12, 3.13, and 4.2.

"Judicial candidate" means any person, including a sitting judge, who is seeking selection for or retention in judicial office by election or appointment. A person becomes a candidate for judicial office as soon as he or she makes a public announcement of candidacy, declares or files as a candidate with the election or appointment authority, authorizes or, where permitted, engages in solicitation or acceptance of contributions or support, or is nominated for election or appointment to office. See Rules 2.11, 4.1, 4.2, and 4.4.

"Knowingly," "knowledge," "known," and **"knows"** mean actual knowledge of the fact in question. A person's knowledge may be inferred from circumstances. See Rules 2.11, 2.13, 2.15, 2.16, 3.6, and 4.1.

"Law" encompasses court rules as well as statutes, constitutional provisions, and decisional law. See Rules 1.1, 2.1, 2.2, 2.6, 2.7, 2.9, 3.1, 3.4, 3.9, 3.12, 3.13, 3.14, 3.15, 4.1, 4.2, 4.4, and 4.5.

"Member of the candidate's family" means a spouse, domestic partner, child, grandchild, parent, grandparent, or other relative or person with whom the candidate maintains a close familial relationship.

"Member of the judge's family" means a spouse, domestic partner, child, grandchild, parent, grandparent, or other relative or person with whom the judge maintains a close familial relationship. See Rules 3.7, 3.8, 3.10, and 3.11.

"Member of a judge's family residing in the judge's household" means any relative of a judge by blood or marriage, or a person treated by a judge as a member of the judge's family, who resides in the judge's household. See Rules 2.11 and 3.13.

"Nonpublic information" means information that is not available to the public. Nonpublic information may include, but is not limited to, information that is sealed by statute or court order or impounded or communicated in camera, and information offered in grand jury proceedings, presentencing reports, dependency cases, or psychiatric reports. See Rule 3.5.

"Pending matter" is a matter that has commenced. A matter continues to be pending through any appellate process until final disposition. See Rules 2.9, 2.10, 3.13, and 4.1.

"Personally solicit" means a direct request made by a judge or a judicial candidate for financial support or in-kind services, whether made by letter, telephone, or any other means of communication. See Rules 3.7, and 4.1.

"Political organization" means a political party or other group sponsored by or affiliated with a political party or candidate, the principal purpose of which is to further the election or appointment of candidates for political office. For purposes of this Code, the term does not include a judicial candidate's campaign committee created as authorized by Rule 4.4. See Rules 4.1 and 4.2.

"Public election" includes primary and general elections, partisan elections, nonpartisan elections, and retention elections. See Rules 4.2 and 4.4.

"Third degree of relationship" includes the following persons: great-grandparent, grandparent, parent, uncle, aunt, brother, sister, child, grandchild, great-grandchild, nephew, and niece. See Rule 2.11.

Application

The Application section establishes when the various Rules apply to a judge or judicial candidate.

I. **Applicability of This Code**
   (A) **The provisions of the Code apply to all full-time judges. Parts II through V of this section identify provisions that apply to four categories of part-time judges only while they are serving as judges, and provisions that do not apply to part-time judges at any time. All other Rules are therefore applicable to part-time judges at all times. The four categories of judicial service in other than a full-time capacity are necessarily defined in general terms because of the widely varying forms of judicial service. Canon 4 applies to judicial candidates.**
   (B) **A judge, within the meaning of this Code, is anyone who is authorized to perform judicial functions, including an officer such as a justice of the peace, magistrate, court commissioner, special master, referee, or member of the administrative law judiciary.**[1]

Comment

[1] The Rules in this Code have been formulated to address the ethical obligations of any person who serves a judicial function, and are premised upon the supposition that a uniform system of ethical principles should apply to all those authorized to perform judicial functions.

[2] The determination of which category and, accordingly, which specific Rules apply to an individual judicial officer, depends upon the facts of the particular judicial service.

---

1. Each jurisdiction should consider the characteristics of particular positions within the administrative law judiciary in adopting, adapting, applying, and enforcing the Code for the administrative law judiciary. *See, e.g.,* Model Code of Judicial Conduct for Federal Administrative Law Judges (1989) and Model Code of Judicial Conduct for State Administrative Law Judges (1995). Both Model Codes are endorsed by the ABA National Conference of Administrative Law Judiciary.

[3] In recent years many jurisdictions have created what are often called "problem solving" courts, in which judges are authorized by court rules to act in nontraditional ways. For example, judges presiding in drug courts and monitoring the progress of participants in those courts' programs may be authorized and even encouraged to communicate directly with social workers, probation officers, and others outside the context of their usual judicial role as independent decision makers on issues of fact and law. When local rules specifically authorize conduct not otherwise permitted under these Rules, they take precedence over the provisions set forth in the Code. Nevertheless, judges serving on "problem solving" courts shall comply with this Code except to the extent local rules provide and permit otherwise.

II. Retired Judge Subject to Recall

A retired judge subject to recall for service, who by law is not permitted to practice law, is not required to comply:
   (A) with Rule 3.9 (Service as Arbitrator or Mediator), except while serving as a judge.
   (B) at any time with Rule 3.8(A) (Appointments to Fiduciary Positions).

Comment

[1] For the purposes of this section, as long as a retired judge is subject to being recalled for service, the judge is considered to "perform judicial functions."

III. Continuing Part-Time Judge

A judge who serves repeatedly on a part-time basis by election or under a continuing appointment, including a retired judge subject to recall who is permitted to practice law ("continuing part-time judge"),
   (A) is not required to comply:
      (1) with Rule 4.1 (Political and Campaign Activities of Judges and Judicial Candidates in General) (A)(1) through (7), except while serving as a judge; or

(2) at any time with Rules 3.4 (Appointments to Governmental Positions), 3.8(A) (Appointments to Fiduciary Positions), 3.9 (Service as Arbitrator or Mediator), 3.10 (Practice of Law), and 3.11(B) (Financial, Business, or Remunerative Activities); and

(B) shall not practice law in the court on which the judge serves or in any court subject to the appellate jurisdiction of the court on which the judge serves, and shall not act as a lawyer in a proceeding in which the judge has served as a judge or in any other proceeding related thereto.

Comment

[1] When a person who has been a continuing part-time judge is no longer a continuing part-time judge, including a retired judge no longer subject to recall, that person may act as a lawyer in a proceeding in which he or she has served as a judge or in any other proceeding related thereto only with the informed consent of all parties, and pursuant to any applicable Model Rules of Professional Conduct. An adopting jurisdiction should substitute a reference to its applicable rule.

IV. Periodic Part-Time Judge

A periodic part-time judge who serves or expects to serve repeatedly on a part-time basis, but under a separate appointment for each limited period of service or for each matter,

(A) is not required to comply:

(1) with Rule 4.1 (Political and Campaign Activities of Judges and Judicial Candidates in General) (A)(1) through (7), except while serving as a judge; or

(2) at any time with Rules 3.4 (Appointments to Governmental Positions), 3.8(A) (Appointments to Fiduciary Positions), 3.9 (Service as Arbitrator or Mediator), 3.10 (Practice of Law), and 3.11(B) (Financial, Business, or Remunerative Activities); and

(B) shall not practice law in the court on which the judge serves or in any court subject to the appellate jurisdiction of the court on which the judge serves, and shall not act as a lawyer in a proceeding in which the judge has served as a judge or in any other proceeding related thereto.

V. Pro Tempore Part-Time Judge

A pro tempore part-time judge who serves or expects to serve once or only sporadically on a part-time basis under a separate appointment for each period of service or for each case heard is not required to comply:

(A) except while serving as a judge, with Rules 2.4 (External Influences on Judicial Conduct), 3.2 (Appearances before Governmental Bodies and Consultation with Government Officials), and 4.1 (Political and Campaign Activities of Judges and Judicial Candidates in General) (A)(1) through (7); or

(B) at any time with Rules 3.4 (Appointments to Governmental Positions), 3.8(A) (Appointments to Fiduciary Positions), 3.9 (Service as Arbitrator or Mediator), 3.10 (Practice of Law), and 3.11(B) (Financial, Business, or Remunerative Activities).

VI. Time for Compliance

A person to whom this Code becomes applicable shall comply immediately with its provisions, except that those judges to whom Rules 3.8 (Appointments to Fiduciary Positions) and 3.11 (Financial, Business, or Remunerative Activities) apply shall comply with those Rules as soon as reasonably possible, but in no event later than one year after the Code becomes applicable to the judge.

Comment

[1] If serving as a fiduciary when selected as judge, a new judge may, notwithstanding the prohibitions in Rule 3.8, continue to serve as fiduciary, but only for that period of time necessary to avoid serious

adverse consequences to the beneficiaries of the fiduciary relationship and in no event longer than one year. Similarly, if engaged at the time of judicial selection in a business activity, a new judge may, notwithstanding the prohibitions in Rule 3.11, continue in that activity for a reasonable period but in no event longer than one year.

Canon 1

A JUDGE SHALL UPHOLD AND PROMOTE THE INDEPENDENCE, IN-
TEGRITY, AND IMPARTIALITY OF THE JUDICIARY, AND SHALL AVOID
IMPROPRIETY AND THE APPEARANCE OF IMPROPRIETY.

Rule 1.1: Compliance with the Law

A judge shall comply with the law,* including the Code of Judicial
Conduct.

Rule 1.2: Promoting Confidence in the Judiciary

A judge shall act at all times in a manner that promotes public confidence in the independence,* integrity,* and impartiality* of the
judiciary, and shall avoid impropriety and the appearance of impropriety.

Comment

[1] Public confidence in the judiciary is eroded by improper conduct and conduct that creates the appearance of impropriety. This principle applies to both the professional and personal conduct of a judge.

[2] A judge should expect to be the subject of public scrutiny that
might be viewed as burdensome if applied to other citizens, and must
accept the restrictions imposed by the Code.

[3] Conduct that compromises or appears to compromise the independence, integrity, and impartiality of a judge undermines public confidence in the judiciary. Because it is not practicable to list all such
conduct, the Rule is necessarily cast in general terms.

[4] Judges should participate in activities that promote ethical conduct among judges and lawyers, support professionalism within the judiciary and the legal profession, and promote access to justice for all.

[5] Actual improprieties include violations of law, court rules or provisions of this Code. The test for appearance of impropriety is whether
the conduct would create in reasonable minds a perception that the judge
violated this Code or engaged in other conduct that reflects adversely on

the judge's honesty, impartiality, temperament, or fitness to serve as a judge.

[6] A judge should initiate and participate in community outreach activities for the purpose of promoting public understanding of and confidence in the administration of justice. In conducting such activities, the judge must act in a manner consistent with this Code.

Rule 1.3: Avoiding Abuse of the Prestige of Judicial Office

A judge shall not abuse the prestige of judicial office to advance the personal or economic interests* of the judge or others, or allow others to do so.

Comment

[1] It is improper for a judge to use or attempt to use his or her position to gain personal advantage or deferential treatment of any kind. For example, it would be improper for a judge to allude to his or her judicial status to gain favorable treatment in encounters with traffic officials. Similarly, a judge must not use judicial letterhead to gain an advantage in conducting his or her personal business.

[2] A judge may provide a reference or recommendation for an individual based upon the judge's personal knowledge. The judge may use official letterhead if the judge indicates that the reference is personal and if there is no likelihood that the use of the letterhead would reasonably be perceived as an attempt to exert pressure by reason of the judicial office.

[3] Judges may participate in the process of judicial selection by cooperating with appointing authorities and screening committees, and by responding to inquiries from such entities concerning the professional qualifications of a person being considered for judicial office.

[4] Special considerations arise when judges write or contribute to publications of for-profit entities, whether related or unrelated to the law. A judge should not permit anyone associated with the publication of such materials to exploit the judge's office in a manner that violates this Rule or other applicable law. In contracts for publication of a judge's writing, the judge should retain sufficient control over the advertising to avoid such exploitation.

Canon 2

A JUDGE SHALL PERFORM THE DUTIES OF JUDICIAL OFFICE IMPARTIALLY, COMPETENTLY, AND DILIGENTLY.

Rule 2.1: Giving Precedence to the Duties of Judicial Office

The duties of judicial office, as prescribed by law,* shall take precedence over all of a judge's personal and extrajudicial activities.

Comment

[1] To ensure that judges are available to fulfill their judicial duties, judges must conduct their personal and extrajudicial activities to minimize the risk of conflicts that would result in frequent disqualification. See Canon 3.

[2] Although it is not a duty of judicial office unless prescribed by law, judges are encouraged to participate in activities that promote public understanding of and confidence in the justice system.

Rule 2.2: Impartiality and Fairness

A judge shall uphold and apply the law,* and shall perform all duties of judicial office fairly and impartially.*

Comment

[1] To ensure impartiality and fairness to all parties, a judge must be objective and open-minded.

[2] Although each judge comes to the bench with a unique background and personal philosophy, a judge must interpret and apply the law without regard to whether the judge approves or disapproves of the law in question.

[3] When applying and interpreting the law, a judge sometimes may make good-faith errors of fact or law. Errors of this kind do not violate this Rule.

[4] It is not a violation of this Rule for a judge to make reasonable accommodations to ensure pro se litigants the opportunity to have their matters fairly heard.

Rule 2.3: Bias, Prejudice, and Harassment

(A) A judge shall perform the duties of judicial office, including administrative duties, without bias or prejudice.

(B) A judge shall not, in the performance of judicial duties, by words or conduct manifest bias or prejudice, or engage in harassment, including but not limited to bias, prejudice, or harassment based upon race, sex, gender, religion, national origin, ethnicity, disability, age, sexual orientation, marital status, socioeconomic status, or political affiliation, and shall not permit court staff, court officials, or others subject to the judge's direction and control to do so.

(C) A judge shall require lawyers in proceedings before the court to refrain from manifesting bias or prejudice, or engaging in harassment, based upon attributes including but not limited to race, sex, gender, religion, national origin, ethnicity, disability, age, sexual orientation, marital status, socioeconomic status, or political affiliation, against parties, witnesses, lawyers, or others.

(D) The restrictions of paragraphs (B) and (C) do not preclude judges or lawyers from making legitimate reference to the listed factors, or similar factors, when they are relevant to an issue in a proceeding.

Comment

[1] A judge who manifests bias or prejudice in a proceeding impairs the fairness of the proceeding and brings the judiciary into disrepute.

[2] Examples of manifestations of bias or prejudice include but are not limited to epithets; slurs; demeaning nicknames; negative stereotyping; attempted humor based upon stereotypes; threatening, intimidating, or hostile acts; suggestions of connections between race, ethnicity, or nationality and crime; and irrelevant references to personal characteristics. Even facial expressions and body language can convey to parties and lawyers in the proceeding, jurors, the media, and others an appearance of bias or prejudice. A judge must avoid conduct that may reasonably be perceived as prejudiced or biased.

[3] Harassment, as referred to in paragraphs (B) and (C), is verbal or physical conduct that denigrates or shows hostility or aversion toward a person on bases such as race, sex, gender, religion, national origin, ethnicity, disability, age, sexual orientation, marital status, socioeconomic status, or political affiliation.

[4] Sexual harassment includes but is not limited to sexual advances, requests for sexual favors, and other verbal or physical conduct of a sexual nature that is unwelcome.

Rule 2.4: External Influences
on Judicial Conduct

(A) A judge shall not be swayed by public clamor or fear of criticism.

(B) A judge shall not permit family, social, political, financial, or other interests or relationships to influence the judge's judicial conduct or judgment.

(C) A judge shall not convey or permit others to convey the impression that any person or organization is in a position to influence the judge.

Comment

[1] An independent judiciary requires that judges decide cases according to the law and facts, without regard to whether particular laws or litigants are popular or unpopular with the public, the media, government officials, or the judge's friends or family. Confidence in the judiciary is eroded if judicial decision making is perceived to be subject to inappropriate outside influences.

Rule 2.5: Competence, Diligence,
and Cooperation

(A) A judge shall perform judicial and administrative duties, competently and diligently.

(B) A judge shall cooperate with other judges and court officials in the administration of court business.

Comment

[1] Competence in the performance of judicial duties requires the legal knowledge, skill, thoroughness, and preparation reasonably necessary to perform a judge's responsibilities of judicial office.

[2] A judge should seek the necessary docket time, court staff, expertise, and resources to discharge all adjudicative and administrative responsibilities.

[3] Prompt disposition of the court's business requires a judge to devote adequate time to judicial duties, to be punctual in attending court and expeditious in determining matters under submission, and to take reasonable measures to ensure that court officials, litigants, and their lawyers cooperate with the judge to that end.

[4] In disposing of matters promptly and efficiently, a judge must demonstrate due regard for the rights of parties to be heard and to have issues resolved without unnecessary cost or delay. A judge should monitor and supervise cases in ways that reduce or eliminate dilatory practices, avoidable delays, and unnecessary costs.

Rule 2.6: Ensuring the Right to Be Heard

(A) A judge shall accord to every person who has a legal interest in a proceeding, or that person's lawyer, the right to be heard according to law.*

(B) A judge may encourage parties to a proceeding and their lawyers to settle matters in dispute but shall not act in a manner that coerces any party into settlement.

Comment

[1] The right to be heard is an essential component of a fair and impartial system of justice. Substantive rights of litigants can be protected only if procedures protecting the right to be heard are observed.

[2] The judge plays an important role in overseeing the settlement of disputes, but should be careful that efforts to further settlement do not undermine any party's right to be heard according to law. The judge should keep in mind the effect that the judge's participation in settlement discussions may have, not only on the judge's own views of the case, but

also on the perceptions of the lawyers and the parties if the case remains with the judge after settlement efforts are unsuccessful. Among the factors that a judge should consider when deciding upon an appropriate settlement practice for a case are (1) whether the parties have requested or voluntarily consented to a certain level of participation by the judge in settlement discussions, (2) whether the parties and their counsel are relatively sophisticated in legal matters, (3) whether the case will be tried by the judge or a jury, (4) whether the parties participate with their counsel in settlement discussions, (5) whether any parties are unrepresented by counsel, and (6) whether the matter is civil or criminal.

[3] Judges must be mindful of the effect settlement discussions can have, not only on their objectivity and impartiality, but also on the appearance of their objectivity and impartiality. Despite a judge's best efforts, there may be instances when information obtained during settlement discussions could influence a judge's decision making during trial, and, in such instances, the judge should consider whether disqualification may be appropriate. See Rule 2.11(A)(1).

Rule 2.7: Responsibility to Decide

A judge shall hear and decide matters assigned to the judge, except when disqualification is required by Rule 2.11 or other law.*

Comment

[1] Judges must be available to decide the matters that come before the court. Although there are times when disqualification is necessary to protect the rights of litigants and preserve public confidence in the independence, integrity, and impartiality of the judiciary, judges must be available to decide matters that come before the courts. Unwarranted disqualification may bring public disfavor to the court and to the judge personally. The dignity of the court, the judge's respect for fulfillment of judicial duties, and a proper concern for the burdens that may be imposed upon the judge's colleagues require that a judge not use disqualification to avoid cases that present difficult, controversial, or unpopular issues.

Rule 2.8: Decorum, Demeanor, and Communication with Jurors

(A) A judge shall require order and decorum in proceedings before the court.

(B) A judge shall be patient, dignified, and courteous to litigants, jurors, witnesses, lawyers, court staff, court officials, and others with whom the judge deals in an official capacity, and shall require similar conduct of lawyers, court staff, court officials, and others subject to the judge's direction and control.

(C) A judge shall not commend or criticize jurors for their verdict other than in a court order or opinion in a proceeding.

Comment

[1] The duty to hear all proceedings with patience and courtesy is not inconsistent with the duty imposed in Rule 2.5 to dispose promptly of the business of the court. Judges can be efficient and businesslike while being patient and deliberate.

[2] Commending or criticizing jurors for their verdict may imply a judicial expectation in future cases and may impair a juror's ability to be fair and impartial in a subsequent case.

[3] A judge who is not otherwise prohibited by law from doing so may meet with jurors who choose to remain after trial but should be careful not to discuss the merits of the case.

Rule 2.9: Ex Parte Communications

(A) A judge shall not initiate, permit, or consider ex parte communications, or consider other communications made to the judge outside the presence of the parties or their lawyers, concerning a pending* or impending matter,* except as follows:

(1) When circumstances require it, ex parte communication for scheduling, administrative, or emergency purposes, which does not address substantive matters, is permitted, provided:

(a) the judge reasonably believes that no party will gain a procedural, substantive, or tactical advantage as a result of the ex parte communication; and

(b) the judge makes provision promptly to notify all other parties of the substance of the ex parte communication, and gives the parties an opportunity to respond.

(2) A judge may obtain the written advice of a disinterested expert on the law applicable to a proceeding before the judge, if the judge gives advance notice to the parties of the person to be consulted and the subject matter of the advice to be solicited, and affords the parties a reasonable opportunity to object and respond to the notice and to the advice received.

(3) A judge may consult with court staff and court officials whose functions are to aid the judge in carrying out the judge's adjudicative responsibilities, or with other judges, provided the judge makes reasonable efforts to avoid receiving factual information that is not part of the record, and does not abrogate the responsibility personally to decide the matter.

(4) A judge may, with the consent of the parties, confer separately with the parties and their lawyers in an effort to settle matters pending before the judge.

(5) A judge may initiate, permit, or consider any ex parte communication when expressly authorized by law* to do so.

(B) If a judge inadvertently receives an unauthorized ex parte communication bearing upon the substance of a matter, the judge shall make provision promptly to notify the parties of the substance of the communication and provide the parties with an opportunity to respond.

(C) A judge shall not investigate facts in a matter independently, and shall consider only the evidence presented and any facts that may properly be judicially noticed.

(D) A judge shall make reasonable efforts, including providing appropriate supervision, to ensure that this Rule is not violated by court staff, court officials, and others subject to the judge's direction and control.

Comment

[1] To the extent reasonably possible, all parties or their lawyers shall be included in communications with a judge.

[2] Whenever the presence of a party or notice to a party is required by this Rule, it is the party's lawyer, or if the party is unrepresented, the party, who is to be present or to whom notice is to be given.

[3] The proscription against communications concerning a proceeding includes communications with lawyers, law teachers, and other persons who are not participants in the proceeding, except to the limited extent permitted by this Rule.

[4] A judge may initiate, permit, or consider ex parte communications expressly authorized by law, such as when serving on therapeutic or problem-solving courts, mental health courts, or drug courts. In this capacity, judges may assume a more interactive role with parties, treatment providers, probation officers, social workers, and others.

[5] A judge may consult with other judges on pending matters, but must avoid ex parte discussions of a case with judges who have previously been disqualified from hearing the matter, and with judges who have appellate jurisdiction over the matter.

[6] The prohibition against a judge investigating the facts in a matter extends to information available in all mediums, including electronic.

[7] A judge may consult ethics advisory committees, outside counsel, or legal experts concerning the judge's compliance with this Code. Such consultations are not subject to the restrictions of paragraph (A)(2).

Rule 2.10: Judicial Statements on Pending and Impending Cases

(A) A judge shall not make any public statement that might reasonably be expected to affect the outcome or impair the fairness of a matter pending* or impending* in any court, or make any nonpublic statement that might substantially interfere with a fair trial or hearing.

(B) A judge shall not, in connection with cases, controversies, or issues that are likely to come before the court, make pledges, promises, or commitments that are inconsistent with the impartial* performance of the adjudicative duties of judicial office.

(C) A judge shall require court staff, court officials, and others subject to the judge's direction and control to refrain from making statements that the judge would be prohibited from making by paragraphs (A) and (B).

(D) Notwithstanding the restrictions in paragraph (A), a judge may make public statements in the course of official duties, may explain court procedures, and may comment on any proceeding in which the judge is a litigant in a personal capacity.

(E) Subject to the requirements of paragraph (A), a judge may respond directly or through a third party to allegations in the media or elsewhere concerning the judge's conduct in a matter.

Comment

[1] This Rule's restrictions on judicial speech are essential to the maintenance of the independence, integrity, and impartiality of the judiciary.

[2] This Rule does not prohibit a judge from commenting on proceedings in which the judge is a litigant in a personal capacity, or represents a client as permitted by these Rules. In cases in which the judge is a litigant in an official capacity, such as a writ of mandamus, the judge must not comment publicly.

[3] Depending upon the circumstances, the judge should consider whether it may be preferable for a third party, rather than the judge, to respond or issue statements in connection with allegations concerning the judge's conduct in a matter.

Rule 2.11: Disqualification

(A) A judge shall disqualify himself or herself in any proceeding in which the judge's impartiality* might reasonably be questioned, including but not limited to the following circumstances:

(1) The judge has a personal bias or prejudice concerning a party or a party's lawyer, or personal knowledge* of facts that are in dispute in the proceeding.

(2) The judge knows* that the judge, the judge's spouse or domestic partner,* or a person within the third degree of relationship* to either of them, or the spouse or domestic partner of such a person is:

(a) a party to the proceeding, or an officer, director, general partner, managing member, or trustee of a party;

(b) acting as a lawyer in the proceeding;

(c) a person who has more than a de minimis* interest that could be substantially affected by the proceeding; or

(d) likely to be a material witness in the proceeding.

(3) The judge knows that he or she, individually or as a fiduciary,* or the judge's spouse, domestic partner, parent, or child, or any other member of the judge's family residing in the judge's household,* has an economic interest* in the subject matter in controversy or in a party to the proceeding.

(4) The judge knows or learns by means of a timely motion that a party, a party's lawyer, or the law firm of a party's lawyer has within the previous [insert number] year[s] made aggregate* contributions* to the judge's campaign in an amount that [is greater than $[insert amount] for an individual or $[insert amount] for an entity] [is reasonable and appropriate for an individual or an entity].

(5) The judge, while a judge or a judicial candidate,* has made a public statement, other than in a court proceeding, judicial decision, or opinion, that commits or appears to commit the judge to reach a particular result or rule in a particular way in the proceeding or controversy.

(6) The judge:

(a) served as a lawyer in the matter in controversy, or was associated with a lawyer who participated substantially as a lawyer in the matter during such association;

(b) served in governmental employment, and in such capacity participated personally and substantially as a lawyer or public official concerning the proceeding, or has publicly expressed in such capacity an opinion concerning the merits of the particular matter in controversy;

(c) was a material witness concerning the matter; or

(d) previously presided as a judge over the matter in another court.

(B) A judge shall keep informed about the judge's personal and fiduciary economic interests, and make a reasonable effort to keep informed about the personal economic interests of the judge's spouse or domestic partner and minor children residing in the judge's household.

(C) A judge subject to disqualification under this Rule, other than for bias or prejudice under paragraph (A)(1), may disclose on the record the basis of the judge's disqualification and may ask the parties and their lawyers to consider, outside the presence of the judge and court personnel, whether to waive disqualification. If, following the disclosure, the parties and lawyers agree, without participation by the judge or court personnel, that the judge should not be disqualified, the judge may participate in the proceeding. The agreement shall be incorporated into the record of the proceeding.

Comment

[1] Under this Rule, a judge is disqualified whenever the judge's impartiality might reasonably be questioned, regardless of whether any of the specific provisions of paragraphs (A)(1) through (6) apply. In many jurisdictions, the term "recusal" is used interchangeably with the term "disqualification."

[2] A judge's obligation not to hear or decide matters in which disqualification is required applies regardless of whether a motion to disqualify is filed.

[3] The rule of necessity may override the rule of disqualification. For example, a judge might be required to participate in judicial review of a judicial salary statute, or might be the only judge available in a matter requiring immediate judicial action, such as a hearing on probable cause or a temporary restraining order. In matters that require immediate action, the judge must disclose on the record the basis for possible disqualification and make reasonable efforts to transfer the matter to another judge as soon as practicable.

[4] The fact that a lawyer in a proceeding is affiliated with a law firm with which a relative of the judge is affiliated does not itself disqualify the judge. If, however, the judge's impartiality might reasonably be questioned under paragraph (A), or the relative is known by the judge to have an interest in the law firm that could be substantially affected by

the proceeding under paragraph (A)(2)(c), the judge's disqualification is required.

[5] A judge should disclose on the record information that the judge believes the parties or their lawyers might reasonably consider relevant to a possible motion for disqualification, even if the judge believes there is no basis for disqualification.

[6] "Economic interest," as set forth in the Terminology section, means ownership of more than a de minimis legal or equitable interest. Except for situations in which a judge participates in the management of such a legal or equitable interest, or the interest could be substantially affected by the outcome of a proceeding before a judge, it does not include:

(1) an interest in the individual holdings within a mutual or common investment fund;

(2) an interest in securities held by an educational, religious, charitable, fraternal, or civic organization in which the judge or the judge's spouse, domestic partner, parent, or child serves as a director, officer, advisor, or other participant;

(3) a deposit in a financial institution or deposits or proprietary interests the judge may maintain as a member of a mutual savings association or credit union, or similar proprietary interests; or

(4) an interest in the issuer of government securities held by the judge.

Rule 2.12: Supervisory Duties

(A) A judge shall require court staff, court officials, and others subject to the judge's direction and control to act in a manner consistent with the judge's obligations under this Code.

(B) A judge with supervisory authority for the performance of other judges shall take reasonable measures to ensure that those judges properly discharge their judicial responsibilities, including the prompt disposition of matters before them.

Comment

[1] A judge is responsible for his or her own conduct and for the conduct of others, such as staff, when those persons are acting at the judge's direction or control. A judge may not direct court personnel to engage in conduct on the judge's behalf or as the judge's representative when such conduct would violate the Code if undertaken by the judge.

[2] Public confidence in the judicial system depends upon timely justice. To promote the efficient administration of justice, a judge with supervisory authority must take the steps needed to ensure that judges under his or her supervision administer their workloads promptly.

Rule 2.13: Administrative Appointments

(A) In making administrative appointments, a judge:
   (1) shall exercise the power of appointment impartially* and on the basis of merit; and
   (2) shall avoid nepotism, favoritism, and unnecessary appointments.

(B) A judge shall not appoint a lawyer to a position if the judge either knows* that the lawyer, or the lawyer's spouse or domestic partner,* has contributed more than $[insert amount] within the prior [insert number] year[s] to the judge's election campaign, or learns of such a contribution* by means of a timely motion by a party or other person properly interested in the matter, unless:
   (1) the position is substantially uncompensated;
   (2) the lawyer has been selected in rotation from a list of qualified and available lawyers compiled without regard to their having made political contributions; or
   (3) the judge or another presiding or administrative judge affirmatively finds that no other lawyer is willing, competent, and able to accept the position.

(C) A judge shall not approve compensation of appointees beyond the fair value of services rendered.

Comment

[1] Appointees of a judge include assigned counsel, officials such as referees, commissioners, special masters, receivers, and guardians,

and personnel such as clerks, secretaries, and bailiffs. Consent by the parties to an appointment or an award of compensation does not relieve the judge of the obligation prescribed by paragraph (A).

[2] Unless otherwise defined by law, nepotism is the appointment or hiring of any relative within the third degree of relationship of either the judge or the judge's spouse or domestic partner, or the spouse or domestic partner of such relative.

[3] The rule against making administrative appointments of lawyers who have contributed in excess of a specified dollar amount to a judge's election campaign includes an exception for positions that are substantially uncompensated, such as those for which the lawyer's compensation is limited to reimbursement for out-of-pocket expenses.

Rule 2.14: Disability and Impairment

A judge having a reasonable belief that the performance of a lawyer or another judge is impaired by drugs or alcohol, or by a mental, emotional, or physical condition, shall take appropriate action, which may include a confidential referral to a lawyer or judicial assistance program.

Comment

[1] "Appropriate action" means action intended and reasonably likely to help the judge or lawyer in question address the problem and prevent harm to the justice system. Depending upon the circumstances, appropriate action may include but is not limited to speaking directly to the impaired person, notifying an individual with supervisory responsibility over the impaired person, or making a referral to an assistance program.

[2] Taking or initiating corrective action by way of referral to an assistance program may satisfy a judge's responsibility under this Rule. Assistance programs have many approaches for offering help to impaired judges and lawyers, such as intervention, counseling, or referral to appropriate health care professionals. Depending upon the gravity of the conduct that has come to the judge's attention, however, the judge may be required to take other action, such as reporting the impaired judge or lawyer to the appropriate authority, agency, or body. See Rule 2.15.

Rule 2.15: Responding to Judicial and Lawyer Misconduct

(A) A judge having knowledge* that another judge has committed a violation of this Code that raises a substantial question regarding the judge's honesty, trustworthiness, or fitness as a judge in other respects shall inform the appropriate authority.*

(B) A judge having knowledge that a lawyer has committed a violation of the Rules of Professional Conduct that raises a substantial question regarding the lawyer's honesty, trustworthiness, or fitness as a lawyer in other respects shall inform the appropriate authority.

(C) A judge who receives information indicating a substantial likelihood that another judge has committed a violation of this Code shall take appropriate action.

(D) A judge who receives information indicating a substantial likelihood that a lawyer has committed a violation of the Rules of Professional Conduct shall take appropriate action.

Comment

[1] Taking action to address known misconduct is a judge's obligation. Paragraphs (A) and (B) impose an obligation on the judge to report to the appropriate disciplinary authority the known misconduct of another judge or a lawyer that raises a substantial question regarding the honesty, trustworthiness, or fitness of that judge or lawyer. Ignoring or denying known misconduct among one's judicial colleagues or members of the legal profession undermines a judge's responsibility to participate in efforts to ensure public respect for the justice system. This Rule limits the reporting obligation to those offenses that an independent judiciary must vigorously endeavor to prevent.

[2] A judge who does not have actual knowledge that another judge or a lawyer may have committed misconduct, but receives information indicating a substantial likelihood of such misconduct, is required to take appropriate action under paragraphs (C) and (D). Appropriate action may include, but is not limited to, communicating directly with the judge who may have violated this Code, communicating with a supervising judge, or reporting the suspected violation to the appropriate authority or other agency or body. Similarly, actions to be taken in response to information indicating that a lawyer has committed a violation of the

Rules of Professional Conduct may include but are not limited to communicating directly with the lawyer who may have committed the violation, or reporting the suspected violation to the appropriate authority or other agency or body.

Rule 2.16: Cooperation with Disciplinary Authorities

(A) A judge shall cooperate and be candid and honest with judicial and lawyer disciplinary agencies.

(B) A judge shall not retaliate, directly or indirectly, against a person known* or suspected to have assisted or cooperated with an investigation of a judge or a lawyer.

Comment

[1] Cooperation with investigations and proceedings of judicial and lawyer discipline agencies, as required in paragraph (A), instills confidence in judges' commitment to the integrity of the judicial system and the protection of the public.

Canon 3

A JUDGE SHALL CONDUCT THE JUDGE'S PERSONAL AND EXTRAJU-
DICIAL ACTIVITIES TO MINIMIZE THE RISK OF CONFLICT WITH THE
OBLIGATIONS OF JUDICIAL OFFICE.

Rule 3.1: Extrajudicial Activities in General

A judge may engage in extrajudicial activities, except as prohibited by law* or this Code. However, when engaging in extrajudicial activities, a judge shall not:

(A) participate in activities that will interfere with the proper performance of the judge's judicial duties;

(B) participate in activities that will lead to frequent disqualification of the judge;

(C) participate in activities that would appear to a reasonable person to undermine the judge's independence,* integrity,* or impartiality;*

(D) engage in conduct that would appear to a reasonable person to be coercive; or

(E) make use of court premises, staff, stationery, equipment, or other resources, except for incidental use for activities that concern the law, the legal system, or the administration of justice, or unless such additional use is permitted by law.

Comment

[1] To the extent that time permits, and judicial independence and impartiality are not compromised, judges are encouraged to engage in appropriate extrajudicial activities. Judges are uniquely qualified to engage in extrajudicial activities that concern the law, the legal system, and the administration of justice, such as by speaking, writing, teaching, or participating in scholarly research projects. In addition, judges are permitted and encouraged to engage in educational, religious, charitable, fraternal or civic extrajudicial activities not conducted for profit, even when the activities do not involve the law. See Rule 3.7.

[2] Participation in both law-related and other extrajudicial activities helps integrate judges into their communities, and furthers public understanding of and respect for courts and the judicial system.

[3] Discriminatory actions and expressions of bias or prejudice by a judge, even outside the judge's official or judicial actions, are likely to appear to a reasonable person to call into question the judge's integrity and impartiality. Examples include jokes or other remarks that demean individuals based upon their race, sex, gender, religion, national origin, ethnicity, disability, age, sexual orientation, or socioeconomic status. For the same reason, a judge's extrajudicial activities must not be conducted in connection or affiliation with an organization that practices invidious discrimination. See Rule 3.6.

[4] While engaged in permitted extrajudicial activities, judges must not coerce others or take action that would reasonably be perceived as coercive. For example, depending upon the circumstances, a judge's solicitation of contributions or memberships for an organization, even as permitted by Rule 3.7(A), might create the risk that the person solicited would feel obligated to respond favorably, or would do so to curry favor with the judge.

Rule 3.2: Appearances before Governmental Bodies and Consultation with Government Officials

A judge shall not appear voluntarily at a public hearing before, or otherwise consult with, an executive or a legislative body or official, except:

(A) in connection with matters concerning the law, the legal system, or the administration of justice;

(B) in connection with matters about which the judge acquired knowledge or expertise in the course of the judge's judicial duties; or

(C) when the judge is acting pro se in a matter involving the judge's legal or economic interests, or when the judge is acting in a fiduciary* capacity.

Comment

[1] Judges possess special expertise in matters of law, the legal system, and the administration of justice, and may properly share that ex-

pertise with governmental bodies and executive or legislative branch officials.

[2] In appearing before governmental bodies or consulting with government officials, judges must be mindful that they remain subject to other provisions of this Code, such as Rule 1.3, prohibiting judges from using the prestige of office to advance their own or others' interests, Rule 2.10, governing public comment on pending and impending matters, and Rule 3.1(C), prohibiting judges from engaging in extrajudicial activities that would appear to a reasonable person to undermine the judge's independence, integrity, or impartiality.

[3] In general, it would be an unnecessary and unfair burden to prohibit judges from appearing before governmental bodies or consulting with government officials on matters that are likely to affect them as private citizens, such as zoning proposals affecting their real property. In engaging in such activities, however, judges must not refer to their judicial positions, and must otherwise exercise caution to avoid using the prestige of judicial office.

Rule 3.3: Testifying as a Character Witness

A judge shall not testify as a character witness in a judicial, administrative, or other adjudicatory proceeding or otherwise vouch for the character of a person in a legal proceeding, except when duly summoned.

Comment

[1] A judge who, without being subpoenaed, testifies as a character witness abuses the prestige of judicial office to advance the interests of another. See Rule 1.3. Except in unusual circumstances where the demands of justice require, a judge should discourage a party from requiring the judge to testify as a character witness.

Rule 3.4: Appointments to Governmental Positions

A judge shall not accept appointment to a governmental committee, board, commission, or other governmental position, unless it is one that concerns the law, the legal system, or the administration of justice.

Comment

[1] Rule 3.4 implicitly acknowledges the value of judges accepting appointments to entities that concern the law, the legal system, or the administration of justice. Even in such instances, however, a judge should assess the appropriateness of accepting an appointment, paying particular attention to the subject matter of the appointment and the availability and allocation of judicial resources, including the judge's time commitments, and giving due regard to the requirements of the independence and impartiality of the judiciary.

[2] A judge may represent his or her country, state, or locality on ceremonial occasions or in connection with historical, educational, or cultural activities. Such representation does not constitute acceptance of a government position.

Rule 3.5: Use of Nonpublic Information

A judge shall not intentionally disclose or use nonpublic information* acquired in a judicial capacity for any purpose unrelated to the judge's judicial duties.

Comment

[1] In the course of performing judicial duties, a judge may acquire information of commercial or other value that is unavailable to the public. The judge must not reveal or use such information for personal gain or for any purpose unrelated to his or her judicial duties.

[2] This rule is not intended, however, to affect a judge's ability to act on information as necessary to protect the health or safety of the judge or a member of a judge's family, court personnel, or other judicial officers if consistent with other provisions of this Code.

Rule 3.6: Affiliation with Discriminatory Organizations

(A) A judge shall not hold membership in any organization that practices invidious discrimination on the basis of race, sex, gender, religion, national origin, ethnicity, or sexual orientation.

(B) A judge shall not use the benefits or facilities of an organization if the judge knows* or should know that the organization practices invidious discrimination on one or more of the bases identified in paragraph (A). A judge's attendance at an event in a facility of an organization that the judge is not permitted to join is not a violation of this Rule when the judge's attendance is an isolated event that could not reasonably be perceived as an endorsement of the organization's practices.

Comment

[1] A judge's public manifestation of approval of invidious discrimination on any basis gives rise to the appearance of impropriety and diminishes public confidence in the integrity and impartiality of the judiciary. A judge's membership in an organization that practices invidious discrimination creates the perception that the judge's impartiality is impaired.

[2] An organization is generally said to discriminate invidiously if it arbitrarily excludes from membership on the basis of race, sex, gender, religion, national origin, ethnicity, or sexual orientation persons who would otherwise be eligible for admission. Whether an organization practices invidious discrimination is a complex question to which judges should be attentive. The answer cannot be determined from a mere examination of an organization's current membership rolls, but rather, depends upon how the organization selects members, as well as other relevant factors, such as whether the organization is dedicated to the preservation of religious, ethnic, or cultural values of legitimate common interest to its members, or whether it is an intimate, purely private organization whose membership limitations could not constitutionally be prohibited.

[3] When a judge learns that an organization to which the judge belongs engages in invidious discrimination, the judge must resign immediately from the organization.

[4] A judge's membership in a religious organization as a lawful exercise of the freedom of religion is not a violation of this Rule.

[5] This Rule does not apply to national or state military service.

Rule 3.7: Participation in Educational, Religious, Charitable, Fraternal, or Civic Organizations and Activities

(A) Subject to the requirements of Rule 3.1, a judge may participate in activities sponsored by organizations or governmental entities concerned with the law, the legal system, or the administration of justice, and those sponsored by or on behalf of educational, religious, charitable, fraternal, or civic organizations not conducted for profit, including but not limited to the following activities:

(1) assisting such an organization or entity in planning related to fund-raising, and participating in the management and investment of the organization's or entity's funds;

(2) soliciting* contributions* for such an organization or entity, but only from members of the judge's family,* or from judges over whom the judge does not exercise supervisory or appellate authority;

(3) soliciting membership for such an organization or entity, even though the membership dues or fees generated may be used to support the objectives of the organization or entity, but only if the organization or entity is concerned with the law, the legal system, or the administration of justice;

(4) appearing or speaking at, receiving an award or other recognition at, being featured on the program of, and permitting his or her title to be used in connection with an event of such an organization or entity, but if the event serves a fund-raising purpose, the judge may participate only if the event concerns the law, the legal system, or the administration of justice;

(5) making recommendations to such a public or private fund-granting organization or entity in connection with its programs and activities, but only if the organization or entity is concerned with the law, the legal system, or the administration of justice; and

(6) serving as an officer, director, trustee, or nonlegal advisor of such an organization or entity, unless it is likely that the organization or entity:

(a) **will be engaged in proceedings that would ordinarily come before the judge; or**
(b) **will frequently be engaged in adversary proceedings in the court of which the judge is a member, or in any court subject to the appellate jurisdiction of the court of which the judge is a member.**

(B) **A judge may encourage lawyers to provide pro bono publico legal services.**

Comment

[1] The activities permitted by paragraph (A) generally include those sponsored by or undertaken on behalf of public or private not-for-profit educational institutions, and other not-for-profit organizations, including law-related, charitable, and other organizations.

[2] Even for law-related organizations, a judge should consider whether the membership and purposes of the organization, or the nature of the judge's participation in or association with the organization, would conflict with the judge's obligation to refrain from activities that reflect adversely upon a judge's independence, integrity, and impartiality.

[3] Mere attendance at an event, whether or not the event serves a fund-raising purpose, does not constitute a violation of paragraph (A)(4). It is also generally permissible for a judge to serve as an usher or a food server or preparer, or to perform similar functions, at fund-raising events sponsored by educational, religious, charitable, fraternal, or civic organizations. Such activities are not solicitation and do not present an element of coercion or abuse the prestige of judicial office.

[4] Identification of a judge's position in educational, religious, charitable, fraternal, or civic organizations on letterhead used for fund-raising or membership solicitation does not violate this Rule. The letterhead may list the judge's title or judicial office if comparable designations are used for other persons.

[5] In addition to appointing lawyers to serve as counsel for indigent parties in individual cases, a judge may promote broader access to justice by encouraging lawyers to participate in pro bono publico legal services, if in doing so the judge does not employ coercion, or abuse the prestige of judicial office. Such encouragement may take many forms, including providing lists of available programs, training lawyers to do

pro bono publico legal work, and participating in events recognizing lawyers who have done pro bono publico work.

Rule 3.8: Appointments to Fiduciary Positions

(A) A judge shall not accept appointment to serve in a fiduciary* position, such as executor, administrator, trustee, guardian, attorney in fact, or other personal representative, except for the estate, trust, or person of a member of the judge's family,* and then only if such service will not interfere with the proper performance of judicial duties.

(B) A judge shall not serve in a fiduciary position if the judge as fiduciary will likely be engaged in proceedings that would ordinarily come before the judge, or if the estate, trust, or ward becomes involved in adversary proceedings in the court on which the judge serves, or one under its appellate jurisdiction.

(C) A judge acting in a fiduciary capacity shall be subject to the same restrictions on engaging in financial activities that apply to a judge personally.

(D) If a person who is serving in a fiduciary position becomes a judge, he or she must comply with this Rule as soon as reasonably practicable, but in no event later than [one year] after becoming a judge.

Comment

[1] A judge should recognize that other restrictions imposed by this Code may conflict with a judge's obligations as a fiduciary; in such circumstances, a judge should resign as fiduciary. For example, serving as a fiduciary might require frequent disqualification of a judge under Rule 2.11 because a judge is deemed to have an economic interest in shares of stock held by a trust if the amount of stock held is more than de minimis.

Rule 3.9: Service as Arbitrator or Mediator

A judge shall not act as an arbitrator or a mediator or perform other judicial functions apart from the judge's official duties unless expressly authorized by law.*

Comment

[1] This Rule does not prohibit a judge from participating in arbitration, mediation, or settlement conferences performed as part of assigned judicial duties. Rendering dispute resolution services apart from those duties, whether or not for economic gain, is prohibited unless it is expressly authorized by law.

Rule 3.10: Practice of Law

A judge shall not practice law. A judge may act pro se and may, without compensation, give legal advice to and draft or review documents for a member of the judge's family,* but is prohibited from serving as the family member's lawyer in any forum.

Comment

[1] A judge may act pro se in all legal matters, including matters involving litigation and matters involving appearances before or other dealings with governmental bodies. A judge must not use the prestige of office to advance the judge's personal or family interests. See Rule 1.3.

Rule 3.11: Financial, Business, or Remunerative Activities

(A) A judge may hold and manage investments of the judge and members of the judge's family.*

(B) A judge shall not serve as an officer, director, manager, general partner, advisor, or employee of any business entity except that a judge may manage or participate in:

> **(1) a business closely held by the judge or members of the judge's family; or**
>
> **(2) a business entity primarily engaged in investment of the financial resources of the judge or members of the judge's family.**

(C) A judge shall not engage in financial activities permitted under paragraphs (A) and (B) if they will:

(1) interfere with the proper performance of judicial duties;
(2) lead to frequent disqualification of the judge;
(3) involve the judge in frequent transactions or continuing business relationships with lawyers or other persons likely to come before the court on which the judge serves; or
(4) result in violation of other provisions of this Code.

Comment

[1] Judges are generally permitted to engage in financial activities, including managing real estate and other investments for themselves or for members of their families. Participation in these activities, like participation in other extrajudicial activities, is subject to the requirements of this Code. For example, it would be improper for a judge to spend so much time on business activities that it interferes with the performance of judicial duties. See Rule 2.1. Similarly, it would be improper for a judge to use his or her official title or appear in judicial robes in business advertising, or to conduct his or her business or financial affairs in such a way that disqualification is frequently required. See Rules 1.3 and 2.11.

[2] As soon as practicable without serious financial detriment, the judge must divest himself or herself of investments and other financial interests that might require frequent disqualification or otherwise violate this Rule.

Rule 3.12: Compensation for Extrajudicial Activities

A judge may accept reasonable compensation for extrajudicial activities permitted by this Code or other law* unless such acceptance would appear to a reasonable person to undermine the judge's independence,* integrity,* or impartiality.*

Comment

[1] A judge is permitted to accept honoraria, stipends, fees, wages, salaries, royalties, or other compensation for speaking, teaching, writing, and other extrajudicial activities, provided the compensation is reasonable and commensurate with the task performed. The judge should

be mindful, however, that judicial duties must take precedence over other activities. See Rule 2.1.

[2] Compensation derived from extrajudicial activities may be subject to public reporting. See Rule 3.15.

Rule 3.13: Acceptance and Reporting of Gifts, Loans, Bequests, Benefits, or Other Things of Value

(A) A judge shall not accept any gifts, loans, bequests, benefits, or other things of value, if acceptance is prohibited by law* or would appear to a reasonable person to undermine the judge's independence,* integrity,* or impartiality.*

(B) Unless otherwise prohibited by law, or by paragraph (A), a judge may accept the following without publicly reporting such acceptance:

    (1) items with little intrinsic value, such as plaques, certificates, trophies, and greeting cards;

    (2) gifts, loans, bequests, benefits, or other things of value from friends, relatives, or other persons, including lawyers, whose appearance or interest in a proceeding pending* or impending* before the judge would in any event require disqualification of the judge under Rule 2.11;

    (3) ordinary social hospitality;

    (4) commercial or financial opportunities and benefits, including special pricing and discounts, and loans from lending institutions in their regular course of business, if the same opportunities and benefits or loans are made available on the same terms to similarly situated persons who are not judges;

    (5) rewards and prizes given to competitors or participants in random drawings, contests, or other events that are open to persons who are not judges;

    (6) scholarships, fellowships, and similar benefits or awards, if they are available to similarly situated persons who are not judges, based upon the same terms and criteria;

    (7) books, magazines, journals, audiovisual materials, and other resource materials supplied by publishers on a complimentary basis for official use; or

(8) gifts, awards, or benefits associated with the business, profession, or other separate activity of a spouse, a domestic partner,* or other family member of a judge residing in the judge's household,* but that incidentally benefit the judge.

(C) Unless otherwise prohibited by law or by paragraph (A), a judge may accept the following items, and must report such acceptance to the extent required by Rule 3.15:

(1) gifts incident to a public testimonial;

(2) invitations to the judge and the judge's spouse, domestic partner, or guest to attend without charge:

    (a) an event associated with a bar-related function or other activity relating to the law, the legal system, or the administration of justice; or

    (b) an event associated with any of the judge's educational, religious, charitable, fraternal or civic activities permitted by this Code, if the same invitation is offered to nonjudges who are engaged in similar ways in the activity as is the judge; and

(3) gifts, loans, bequests, benefits, or other things of value, if the source is a party or other person, including a lawyer, who has come or is likely to come before the judge, or whose interests have come or are likely to come before the judge.

Comment

[1] Whenever a judge accepts a gift or other thing of value without paying fair market value, there is a risk that the benefit might be viewed as intended to influence the judge's decision in a case. Rule 3.13 imposes restrictions upon the acceptance of such benefits, according to the magnitude of the risk. Paragraph (B) identifies circumstances in which the risk that the acceptance would appear to undermine the judge's independence, integrity, or impartiality is low, and explicitly provides that such items need not be publicly reported. As the value of the benefit or the likelihood that the source of the benefit will appear before the judge increases, the judge is either prohibited under paragraph (A) from accepting the gift, or required under paragraph (C) to publicly report it.

[2] Gift-giving between friends and relatives is a common occurrence, and ordinarily does not create an appearance of impropriety or cause reasonable persons to believe that the judge's independence, integrity, or impartiality has been compromised. In addition, when the appearance of friends or relatives in a case would require the judge's disqualification under Rule 2.11, there would be no opportunity for a gift to influence the judge's decision making. Paragraph (B)(2) places no restrictions upon the ability of a judge to accept gifts or other things of value from friends or relatives under these circumstances, and does not require public reporting.

[3] Businesses and financial institutions frequently make available special pricing, discounts, and other benefits, either in connection with a temporary promotion or for preferred customers, based upon longevity of the relationship, volume of business transacted, and other factors. A judge may freely accept such benefits if they are available to the general public, or if the judge qualifies for the special price or discount according to the same criteria as are applied to persons who are not judges. As an example, loans provided at generally prevailing interest rates are not gifts, but a judge could not accept a loan from a financial institution at below-market interest rates unless the same rate was being made available to the general public for a certain period of time or only to borrowers with specified qualifications that the judge also possesses.

[4] Rule 3.13 applies only to acceptance of gifts or other things of value by a judge. Nonetheless, if a gift or other benefit is given to the judge's spouse, domestic partner, or member of the judge's family residing in the judge's household, it may be viewed as an attempt to evade Rule 3.13 and influence the judge indirectly. Where the gift or benefit is being made primarily to such other persons, and the judge is merely an incidental beneficiary, this concern is reduced. A judge should, however, remind family and household members of the restrictions imposed upon judges, and urge them to take these restrictions into account when making decisions about accepting such gifts or benefits.

[5] Rule 3.13 does not apply to contributions to a judge's campaign for judicial office. Such contributions are governed by other Rules of this Code, including Rules 4.3 and 4.4.

Rule 3.14: Reimbursement of Expenses and Waivers of Fees or Charges

(A) Unless otherwise prohibited by Rules 3.1 and 3.13(A) or other law,* a judge may accept reimbursement of necessary and reasonable expenses for travel, food, lodging, or other incidental expenses, or a waiver or partial waiver of fees or charges for registration, tuition, and similar items, from sources other than the judge's employing entity, if the expenses or charges are associated with the judge's participation in extrajudicial activities permitted by this Code.

(B) Reimbursement of expenses for necessary travel, food, lodging, or other incidental expenses shall be limited to the actual costs reasonably incurred by the judge and, when appropriate to the occasion, by the judge's spouse, domestic partner,* or guest.

(C) A judge who accepts reimbursement of expenses or waivers or partial waivers of fees or charges on behalf of the judge or the judge's spouse, domestic partner, or guest shall publicly report such acceptance as required by Rule 3.15.

Comment

[1] Educational, civic, religious, fraternal, and charitable organizations often sponsor meetings, seminars, symposia, dinners, awards ceremonies, and similar events. Judges are encouraged to attend educational programs, as both teachers and participants, in law-related and academic disciplines, in furtherance of their duty to remain competent in the law. Participation in a variety of other extrajudicial activity is also permitted and encouraged by this Code.

[2] Not infrequently, sponsoring organizations invite certain judges to attend seminars or other events on a fee-waived or partial-fee-waived basis, and sometimes include reimbursement for necessary travel, food, lodging, or other incidental expenses. A judge's decision whether to accept reimbursement of expenses or a waiver or partial waiver of fees or charges in connection with these or other extrajudicial activities must be based upon an assessment of all the circumstances. The judge must undertake a reasonable inquiry to obtain the information necessary to make an informed judgment about whether acceptance would be consistent with the requirements of this Code.

[3] A judge must assure himself or herself that acceptance of reimbursement or fee waivers would not appear to a reasonable person to undermine the judge's independence, integrity, or impartiality. The factors that a judge should consider when deciding whether to accept reimbursement or a fee waiver for attendance at a particular activity include:

(a) whether the sponsor is an accredited educational institution or bar association rather than a trade association or a for-profit entity;

(b) whether the funding comes largely from numerous contributors rather than from a single entity and is earmarked for programs with specific content;

(c) whether the content is related or unrelated to the subject matter of litigation pending or impending before the judge, or to matters that are likely to come before the judge;

(d) whether the activity is primarily educational rather than recreational, and whether the costs of the event are reasonable and comparable to those associated with similar events sponsored by the judiciary, bar associations, or similar groups;

(e) whether information concerning the activity and its funding sources is available upon inquiry;

(f) whether the sponsor or source of funding is generally associated with particular parties or interests currently appearing or likely to appear in the judge's court, thus possibly requiring disqualification of the judge under Rule 2.11;

(g) whether differing viewpoints are presented; and

(h) whether a broad range of judicial and nonjudicial participants are invited, whether a large number of participants are invited, and whether the program is designed specifically for judges.

Rule 3.15: Reporting Requirements

(A) A judge shall publicly report the amount or value of:

(1) compensation received for extrajudicial activities as permitted by Rule 3.12;

(2) gifts and other things of value as permitted by Rule 3.13(C), unless the value of such items, alone or in the

aggregate with other items received from the same source in the same calendar year, does not exceed $[insert amount]; and

(3) reimbursement of expenses and waiver of fees or charges permitted by Rule 3.14(A), unless the amount of reimbursement or waiver, alone or in the aggregate with other reimbursements or waivers received from the same source in the same calendar year, does not exceed $[insert amount].

(B) When public reporting is required by paragraph (A), a judge shall report the date, place, and nature of the activity for which the judge received any compensation; the description of any gift, loan, bequest, benefit, or other thing of value accepted; and the source of reimbursement of expenses or waiver or partial waiver of fees or charges.

(C) The public report required by paragraph (A) shall be made at least annually, except that for reimbursement of expenses and waiver or partial waiver of fees or charges, the report shall be made within thirty days following the conclusion of the event or program.

(D) Reports made in compliance with this Rule shall be filed as public documents in the office of the clerk of the court on which the judge serves or other office designated by law,* and, when technically feasible, posted by the court or office personnel on the court's website.

Canon 4

A JUDGE OR CANDIDATE FOR JUDICIAL OFFICE SHALL NOT ENGAGE IN POLITICAL OR CAMPAIGN ACTIVITY THAT IS INCONSISTENT WITH THE INDEPENDENCE, INTEGRITY, OR IMPARTIALITY OF THE JUDICIARY.

Rule 4.1: Political and Campaign Activities of Judges and Judicial Candidates in General

(A) Except as permitted by law,* or by Rules 4.2, 4.3, and 4.4, a judge or a judicial candidate* shall not:

(1) act as a leader in, or hold an office in, a political organization;*

(2) make speeches on behalf of a political organization;

(3) publicly endorse or oppose a candidate for any public office;

(4) solicit funds for, pay an assessment to, or make a contribution* to a political organization or a candidate for public office;

(5) attend or purchase tickets for dinners or other events sponsored by a political organization or a candidate for public office;

(6) publicly identify himself or herself as a candidate of a political organization;

(7) seek, accept, or use endorsements from a political organization;

(8) personally solicit* or accept campaign contributions other than through a campaign committee authorized by Rule 4.4;

(9) use or permit the use of campaign contributions for the private benefit of the judge, the candidate, or others;

(10) use court staff, facilities, or other court resources in a campaign for judicial office;

(11) knowingly,* or with reckless disregard for the truth, make any false or misleading statement;

(12) make any statement that would reasonably be expected to affect the outcome or impair the fairness of a matter pending* or impending* in any court; or

(13) in connection with cases, controversies, or issues that are likely to come before the court, make pledges, promises, or commitments that are inconsistent with the impartial* performance of the adjudicative duties of judicial office.

(B) A judge or judicial candidate shall take reasonable measures to ensure that other persons do not undertake, on behalf of the judge or judicial candidate, any activities prohibited under paragraph (A).

Comment

General Considerations

[1] Even when subject to public election, a judge plays a role different from that of a legislator or executive branch official. Rather than making decisions based upon the expressed views or preferences of the electorate, a judge makes decisions based upon the law and the facts of every case. Therefore, in furtherance of this interest, judges and judicial candidates must, to the greatest extent possible, be free and appear to be free from political influence and political pressure. This Canon imposes narrowly tailored restrictions upon the political and campaign activities of all judges and judicial candidates, taking into account the various methods of selecting judges.

[2] When a person becomes a judicial candidate, this Canon becomes applicable to his or her conduct.

Participation in Political Activities

[3] Public confidence in the independence and impartiality of the judiciary is eroded if judges or judicial candidates are perceived to be subject to political influence. Although judges and judicial candidates may register to vote as members of a political party, they are prohibited by paragraph (A)(1) from assuming leadership roles in political organizations.

[4] Paragraphs (A)(2) and (A)(3) prohibit judges and judicial candidates from making speeches on behalf of political organizations or publicly endorsing or opposing candidates for public office, respectively, to

prevent them from abusing the prestige of judicial office to advance the interests of others. See Rule 1.3. These Rules do not prohibit candidates from campaigning on their own behalf, or from endorsing or opposing candidates for the same judicial office for which they are running. See Rules 4.2(B)(2) and 4.2(B)(3).

[5] Although members of the families of judges and judicial candidates are free to engage in their own political activity, including running for public office, there is no "family exception" to the prohibition in paragraph (A)(3) against a judge or candidate publicly endorsing candidates for public office. A judge or judicial candidate must not become involved in, or publicly associated with, a family member's political activity or campaign for public office. To avoid public misunderstanding, judges and judicial candidates should take, and should urge members of their families to take, reasonable steps to avoid any implication that they endorse any family member's candidacy or other political activity.

[6] Judges and judicial candidates retain the right to participate in the political process as voters in both primary and general elections. For purposes of this Canon, participation in a caucus-type election procedure does not constitute public support for or endorsement of a political organization or candidate, and is not prohibited by paragraphs (A)(2) or (A)(3).

Statements and Comments Made during a Campaign for Judicial Office

[7] Judicial candidates must be scrupulously fair and accurate in all statements made by them and by their campaign committees. Paragraph (A)(11) obligates candidates and their committees to refrain from making statements that are false or misleading, or that omit facts necessary to make the communication considered as a whole not materially misleading.

[8] Judicial candidates are sometimes the subject of false, misleading, or unfair allegations made by opposing candidates, third parties, or the media. For example, false or misleading statements might be made regarding the identity, present position, experience, qualifications, or judicial rulings of a candidate. In other situations, false or misleading allegations may be made that bear upon a candidate's integrity or fitness for judicial office. As long as the candidate does not violate paragraphs

(A)(11), (A)(12), or (A)(13), the candidate may make a factually accurate public response. In addition, when an independent third party has made unwarranted attacks on a candidate's opponent, the candidate may disavow the attacks, and request the third party to cease and desist.

[9] Subject to paragraph (A)(12), a judicial candidate is permitted to respond directly to false, misleading, or unfair allegations made against him or her during a campaign, although it is preferable for someone else to respond if the allegations relate to a pending case.

[10] Paragraph (A)(12) prohibits judicial candidates from making comments that might impair the fairness of pending or impending judicial proceedings. This provision does not restrict arguments or statements to the court or jury by a lawyer who is a judicial candidate, or rulings, statements, or instructions by a judge that may appropriately affect the outcome of a matter.

Pledges, Promises, or Commitments Inconsistent with Impartial Performance of the Adjudicative Duties of Judicial Office

[11] The role of a judge is different from that of a legislator or executive branch official, even when the judge is subject to public election. Campaigns for judicial office must be conducted differently from campaigns for other offices. The narrowly drafted restrictions upon political and campaign activities of judicial candidates provided in Canon 4 allow candidates to conduct campaigns that provide voters with sufficient information to permit them to distinguish between candidates and make informed electoral choices.

[12] Paragraph (A)(13) makes applicable to both judges and judicial candidates the prohibition that applies to judges in Rule 2.10(B), relating to pledges, promises, or commitments that are inconsistent with the impartial performance of the adjudicative duties of judicial office.

[13] The making of a pledge, promise, or commitment is not dependent upon, or limited to, the use of any specific words or phrases; instead, the totality of the statement must be examined to determine if a reasonable person would believe that the candidate for judicial office has specifically undertaken to reach a particular result. Pledges, promises, or commitments must be contrasted with statements or announcements of personal views on legal, political, or other issues, which are not prohibited. When making such statements, a judge should acknowledge

the overarching judicial obligation to apply and uphold the law, without regard to his or her personal views.

[14] A judicial candidate may make campaign promises related to judicial organization, administration, and court management, such as a promise to dispose of a backlog of cases, start court sessions on time, or avoid favoritism in appointments and hiring. A candidate may also pledge to take action outside the courtroom, such as working toward an improved jury selection system, or advocating for more funds to improve the physical plant and amenities of the courthouse.

[15] Judicial candidates may receive questionnaires or requests for interviews from the media and from issue advocacy or other community organizations that seek to learn their views on disputed or controversial legal or political issues. Paragraph (A)(13) does not specifically address judicial responses to such inquiries. Depending upon the wording and format of such questionnaires, candidates' responses might be viewed as pledges, promises, or commitments to perform the adjudicative duties of office other than in an impartial way. To avoid violating paragraph (A)(13), therefore, candidates who respond to media and other inquiries should also give assurances that they will keep an open mind and will carry out their adjudicative duties faithfully and impartially if elected. Candidates who do not respond may state their reasons for not responding, such as the danger that answering might be perceived by a reasonable person as undermining a successful candidate's independence or impartiality, or that it might lead to frequent disqualification. See Rule 2.11.

Rule 4.2: Political and Campaign Activities
of Judicial Candidates in Public Elections

(A) A judicial candidate* in a partisan, nonpartisan, or retention public election* shall:

    (1) act at all times in a manner consistent with the independence,* integrity,* and impartiality* of the judiciary;

    (2) comply with all applicable election, election campaign, and election campaign fund-raising laws and regulations of this jurisdiction;

    (3) review and approve the content of all campaign statements and materials produced by the candidate or his or her

campaign committee, as authorized by Rule 4.4, before their dissemination; and

(4) take reasonable measures to ensure that other persons do not undertake on behalf of the candidate activities, other than those described in Rule 4.4, that the candidate is prohibited from doing by Rule 4.1.

(B) A candidate for elective judicial office may, unless prohibited by law,* and not earlier than [insert amount of time] before the first applicable primary election, caucus, or general or retention election:

(1) establish a campaign committee pursuant to the provisions of Rule 4.4;

(2) speak on behalf of his or her candidacy through any medium, including but not limited to advertisements, websites, or other campaign literature;

(3) publicly endorse or oppose candidates for the same judicial office for which he or she is running;

(4) attend or purchase tickets for dinners or other events sponsored by a political organization* or a candidate for public office;

(5) seek, accept, or use endorsements from any person or organization other than a partisan political organization; and

(6) contribute to a political organization or candidate for public office, but not more than $[insert amount] to any one organization or candidate.

(C) A judicial candidate in a partisan public election may, unless prohibited by law, and not earlier than [insert amount of time] before the first applicable primary election, caucus, or general election:

(1) identify himself or herself as a candidate of a political organization; and

(2) seek, accept, and use endorsements of a political organization.

Comment

[1] Paragraphs (B) and (C) permit judicial candidates in public elections to engage in some political and campaign activities otherwise pro-

hibited by Rule 4.1. Candidates may not engage in these activities earlier than [insert amount of time] before the first applicable electoral event, such as a caucus or a primary election.

[2] Despite paragraphs (B) and (C), judicial candidates for public election remain subject to many of the provisions of Rule 4.1. For example, a candidate continues to be prohibited from soliciting funds for a political organization, knowingly making false or misleading statements during a campaign, or making certain promises, pledges, or commitments related to future adjudicative duties. See Rule 4.1(A), paragraphs (4), (11), and (13).

[3] In partisan public elections for judicial office, a candidate may be nominated by, affiliated with, or otherwise publicly identified or associated with a political organization, including a political party. This relationship may be maintained throughout the period of the public campaign, and may include use of political party or similar designations on campaign literature and on the ballot.

[4] In nonpartisan public elections or retention elections, paragraph (B)(5) prohibits a candidate from seeking, accepting, or using nominations or endorsements from a partisan political organization.

[5] Judicial candidates are permitted to attend or purchase tickets for dinners and other events sponsored by political organizations.

[6] For purposes of paragraph (B)(3), candidates are considered to be running for the same judicial office if they are competing for a single judgeship or if several judgeships on the same court are to be filled as a result of the election. In endorsing or opposing another candidate for a position on the same court, a judicial candidate must abide by the same rules governing campaign conduct and speech as apply to the candidate's own campaign.

[7] Although judicial candidates in nonpartisan public elections are prohibited from running on a ticket or slate associated with a political organization, they may group themselves into slates or other alliances to conduct their campaigns more effectively. Candidates who have grouped themselves together are considered to be running for the same judicial office if they satisfy the conditions described in Comment [6].

Rule 4.3: Activities of Candidates for Appointive Judicial Office

A candidate for appointment to judicial office may:

(A) communicate with the appointing or confirming authority, including any selection, screening, or nominating commission or similar agency; and

(B) seek endorsements for the appointment from any person or organization other than a partisan political organization.

Comment

[1] When seeking support or endorsement, or when communicating directly with an appointing or confirming authority, a candidate for appointive judicial office must not make any pledges, promises, or commitments that are inconsistent with the impartial performance of the adjudicative duties of the office. See Rule 4.1(A)(13).

Rule 4.4: Campaign Committees

(A) A judicial candidate* subject to public election* may establish a campaign committee to manage and conduct a campaign for the candidate, subject to the provisions of this Code. The candidate is responsible for ensuring that his or her campaign committee complies with applicable provisions of this Code and other applicable law.*

(B) A judicial candidate subject to public election shall direct his or her campaign committee:

(1) to solicit and accept only such campaign contributions* as are reasonable, in any event not to exceed, in the aggregate,* $[insert amount] from any individual or $[insert amount] from any entity or organization;

(2) not to solicit or accept contributions for a candidate's current campaign more than [insert amount of time] before the applicable primary election, caucus, or general or retention election, nor more than [insert number] days after the last election in which the candidate participated; and

(3) to comply with all applicable statutory requirements for disclosure and divestiture of campaign contributions, and to file with [name of appropriate regulatory authority] a

report stating the name, address, occupation, and employer of each person who has made campaign contributions to the committee in an aggregate value exceeding $[insert amount]. The report must be filed within [insert number] days following an election, or within such other period as is provided by law.

Comment

[1] Judicial candidates are prohibited from personally soliciting campaign contributions or personally accepting campaign contributions. See Rule 4.1(A)(8). This Rule recognizes that in many jurisdictions, judicial candidates must raise campaign funds to support their candidacies, and permits candidates, other than candidates for appointive judicial office, to establish campaign committees to solicit and accept reasonable financial contributions or in-kind contributions.

[2] Campaign committees may solicit and accept campaign contributions, manage the expenditure of campaign funds, and generally conduct campaigns. Candidates are responsible for compliance with the requirements of election law and other applicable law, and for the activities of their campaign committees.

[3] At the start of a campaign, the candidate must instruct the campaign committee to solicit or accept only such contributions as are reasonable in amount, appropriate under the circumstances, and in conformity with applicable law. Although lawyers and others who might appear before a successful candidate for judicial office are permitted to make campaign contributions, the candidate should instruct his or her campaign committee to be especially cautious in connection with such contributions, so they do not create grounds for disqualification if the candidate is elected to judicial office. See Rule 2.11.

Rule 4.5: Activities of Judges Who Become Candidates for Nonjudicial Office

(A) Upon becoming a candidate for a nonjudicial elective office, a judge shall resign from judicial office, unless permitted by law* to continue to hold judicial office.

(B) Upon becoming a candidate for a nonjudicial appointive office, a judge is not required to resign from judicial office, provided that the judge complies with the other provisions of this Code.

Comment

[1] In campaigns for nonjudicial elective public office, candidates may make pledges, promises, or commitments related to positions they would take and ways they would act if elected to office. Although appropriate in nonjudicial campaigns, this manner of campaigning is inconsistent with the role of a judge, who must remain fair and impartial to all who come before him or her. The potential for misuse of the judicial office, and the political promises that the judge would be compelled to make in the course of campaigning for nonjudicial elective office, together dictate that a judge who wishes to run for such an office must resign upon becoming a candidate.

[2] The "resign to run" rule set forth in paragraph (A) ensures that a judge cannot use the judicial office to promote his or her candidacy, and prevents post-campaign retaliation from the judge in the event the judge is defeated in the election. When a judge is seeking appointive nonjudicial office, however, the dangers are not sufficient to warrant imposing the "resign to run" rule.

APPENDIX A
ABA MODEL CODE OF JUDICIAL CONDUCT
CORRELATION TABLES

1990 Code to 2007 Code

1990 CODE	2007 CODE
Preamble	Preamble and Scope
Terminology	Terminology
Canon 1	Canon 1 (partial)
Canon 1A	Preamble [1]
Canon 2	Canon 1 (partial) and Rule 1.2 (partial)
Canon 2A	Rules 1.1 and 1.2 (partial)
Canon 2B	Rules 1.3, 2.4(B) and (C), 3.1(E) and 3.3
Canon 2C	Rule 3.6(A)

Performing the Duties of Judicial Office	
1990 CODE	**2007 CODE**
Canon 3	Canon 2

Judicial Duties in General	
1990 CODE	**2007 CODE**
Canon 3A	Rule 2.1

Adjudicative Responsibilities	
1990 CODE	**2007 CODE**
Canon 3B(1)	Rule 2.7
Canon 3B(2)	Rules 2.2 (partial), 2.4(A) and 2.5(A) (partial)
Canon 3B(3)	Rule 2.8(A)
Canon 3B(4)	Rule 2.8(B)
Canon 3B(5)	Rule 2.3(A) and (B)
Canon 3B(6)	Rule 2.3(C) and (D)
Canon 3B(7)	Rules 2.6(A) and 2.9(A)
Canon 3B(7)(a)	Rule 2.9(A)(1)

Adjudicative Responsibilities (continued)	
1990 CODE	**2007 CODE**
Canon 3B(7)(a)(i)	Rule 2.9(A)(1)(a)
Canon 3B(7)(a)(ii)	Rule 2.9(A)(1)(b)
Canon 3B(7)(b)	Rule 2.9(A)(2)
Canon 3B(7)(c)	Rule 2.9(A)(3)
Canon 3B(7)(d)	Rule 2.9(A)(4)
Canon 3B(7)(e)	Rule 2.9(A)(5)
Canon 3B(8)	Rule 2.2 (partial), 2.5(A)
Canon 3B(9)	Rule 2.10(A), (C) and (D)
Canon 3B(10)	Rule 2.10(B)
Canon 3B(11)	Rule 2.8(C)
Canon 3B(12)	Rule 3.5
Administrative Responsibilities	
1990 CODE	**2007 CODE**
Canon 3C(1)	Rule 2.5(A) and (B)
Canon 3C(2)	Rule 2.12(A)
Canon 3C(3)	Rule 2.12(B)
Canon 3C(4)	Rule 2.13(A), (A)(1), (A)(2) and (C)
Canon 3C(5)	Rule 2.13(B)
Canon 3C(5)(a)	Rule 2.13(B)(1)
Canon 3C(5)(b)	Rule 2.13(B)(2)
Canon 3C(5)(c)	Rule 2.13(B)(3)
Disciplinary Responsibilities	
1990 CODE	**2007 CODE**
Canon 3D(1)	Rule 2.15(A) and (C)
Canon 3D(2)	Rule 2.15(B) and (D)
Canon 3D(3)	Deleted (See REC to Rule 2.15)

Disqualification	
1990 Code	**2007 Code**
Canon 3E(1)	Rule 2.11(A)
Canon 3E(1)(a)	Rule 2.11(A)(1)
Canon 3E(1)(b)	Rule 2.11(A)(6), (A)(6)(a) and (A)(6)(c)
Canon 3E(1)(c)	Rule 2.11(A)(3)
Canon 3E(1)(d)	Rule 2.11(A)(2)
Canon 3E(1)(d)(i)	Rule 2.11(A)(2)(a)
Canon 3E(1)(d)(ii)	Rule 2.11(A)(2)(b)
Canon 3E(1)(d)(iii)	Rule 2.11(A)(2)(c)
Canon 3E(1)(d)(iv)	Rule 2.11(A)(2)(d)
Canon 3E(1)(e)	Rule 2.11(A)(4)
Canon 3E(1)(f)	Rule 2.11(A)(5)
Canon 3E(2)	Rule 2.11(B)

Remittal of Disqualification	
1990 Code	**2007 Code**
Canon 3F	Rule 2.11(C)

Personal and Extrajudicial Activities	
1990 Code	**2007 Code**
Canon 4	Canon 3

Extrajudicial Activities in General	
1990 Code	**2007 Code**
Canon 4A	Rule 3.1
Canon 4A(1)	Rule 3.1(C)
Canon 4A(2)	Deleted
Canon 4A(3)	Rule 3.1(A)

Avocational Activities	
1990 Code	**2007 Code**
Canon 4B	Deleted (See REC to Comment [1] of Rule 3.1)

Governmental, Civic or Charitable Activities	
1990 CODE	**2007 CODE**
Canon 4C(1)	Rules 3.2 and 3.2(A) and (C)
Canon 4C(2)	Rule 3.4
Canon 4C(3)	Rule 3.7(A)
Canon 4C(3)(a)	Rule 3.7(A)(6)
Canon 4C(3)(a)(i)	Rule 3.7(A)(6)(a)
Canon 4C(3)(a)(ii)	Rule 3.7(A)(6)(b)
Canon 4C(3)(b)(i)	Rule 3.7(A)(1) and (2)
Canon 4C(3)(b)(ii)	Rule 3.7(A)(5)
Canon 4C(3)(b)(iii)	Rule 3.7(A)(3)
Canon 4C(3)(b)(iv)	Deleted

Financial Activities	
1990 CODE	**2007 CODE**
Canon 4D(1)	Rule 3.11(C)
Canon 4D(1)(a)	Deleted (See REC to Rule 3.11)
Canon 4D(1)(b)	Rule 3.11(C)(3)
Canon 4D(2)	Rule 3.11(A) (partial)
Canon 4D(3)	Rule 3.11(B)
Canon 4D(3)(a)	Rule 3.11(B)(1)
Canon 4D(3)(b)	Rule 3.11(B)(2)
Canon 4D(4)	Rule 3.11(C)(2)(3) and Comment [2]
Canon 4D(5)	Rule 3.13(A), (B) and (C)
Canon 4D(5)(a)	Rule 3.13(B)(7), (C)(1), (C)(2) and (C)(2)(a)
Canon 4D(5)(b)	Rule 3.13(B)(8)
Canon 4D(5)(c)	Rule 3.13(B)(3)
Canon 4D(5)(d)	Rule 3.13 Comment [2]
Canon 4D(5)(e)	Rule 3.13(B)(2)
Canon 4D(5)(f)	Rule 3.13(B)(4)
Canon 4D(5)(g)	Rule 3.13(B)(6)
Canon 4D(5)(h)	Rule 3.13(C)(3)

Fiduciary Activities	
1990 CODE	**2007 CODE**
Canon 4E(1)	Rule 3.8(A)
Canon 4E(2)	Rule 3.8(B)
Canon 4E(3)	Rule 3.8(C)

Service as Arbitrator or Mediator	
1990 CODE	**2007 CODE**
Canon 4F	Rule 3.9

Practice of Law	
1990 CODE	**2007 CODE**
Canon 4G	Rule 3.10

Compensation, Reimbursement and Reporting	
1990 CODE	**2007 CODE**
Canon 4H(1)	Rules 3.12 (partial) and 3.14(A)
Canon 4H(1)(a)	Rule 3.12
Canon 4H(1)(b)	Rule 3.14(B)
Canon 4H(2)	Rules 3.14(C) and 3.15
Canon 4I	Deleted (See REC to Rule 3.15)

Political and Campaign Activity	
1990 CODE	**2007 CODE**
Canon 5	Canon 4

All Judges and Candidates	
1990 CODE	**2007 CODE**
Canon 5A(1)	Rule 4.1(A)
Canon 5A(1)(a)	Rule 4.1(A)(1)
Canon 5A(1)(b)	Rule 4.1(A)(3)
Canon 5A(1)(c)	Rule 4.1(A)(2)
Canon 5A(1)(d)	Deleted (See REC to Rule 4.1)
Canon 5A(1)(e)	Rule 4.1(A)(4) and (5)
Canon 5A(2)	Rule 4.5(A) and (B)
Canon 5A(3)(a)	Rules 4.1(B), 4.2(A)(1) and (4)
Canon 5A(3)(b)	Rules 4.1(B) and 4.2(A)(4)
Canon 5A(3)(c)	Rule 4.2(A)(4)
Canon 5A(3)(d)	Rule 4.1(A)(13)
Canon 5A(3)(d)(i)	Rule 4.1(A)(13)
Canon 5A(3)(d)(ii)	Rule 4.1(A)(11) (partial)
Canon 5A(3)(e)	Rule 4.1 Comments [8] and [9]

Candidates Seeking Appointment to Judicial or Other Governmental Office	
1990 CODE	**2007 CODE**
Canon 5B	Rule 4.3
Canon 5B(2)	Deleted
Canon 5B(2)(a)(i)	Rule 4.3(A)
Canon 5B(2)(a)(ii)	Rule 4.3(B)
Canon 5B(2)(a)(iii)	Deleted
Canon 5B(2)(b)	Deleted
Judges and Candidates Subject to Public Election	
1990 CODE	**2007 CODE**
Canon 5C(1)	Rule 4.2(A) and (C)
Canon 5C(1)(a)(i)	Rule 4.2(B)(4)
Canon 5C(1)(a)(ii)	Rule 4.2(C)(1)
Canon 5C(1)(a)(iii)	Rule 4.2(B)(6)
Canon 5C(1)(b)(i)	Rule 4.2(B)(2) (partial)
Canon 5C(1)(b)(ii)	Rule 4.2(B)(2) (partial)
Canon 5C(1)(b)(iii)	Rule 4.2(B)(2) (partial)
Canon 5C(1)(b)(iv)	Rule 4.2(B)(3)
Canon 5C(2)	Rules 4.1(A)(8) and (9), 4.2(B) and (B)(1) and 4.4(A), (B), (B)(1) (partial) and (B)(2)
Canon 5C(3)	Rule 4.4(B)(1)
Canon 5C(4)	Rule 4.4(A) and (B)(3) (partial) and Comments [2] and [3]
Canon 5C(5)	Rule 4.2(B)(3) (partial)
Incumbent Judges	
1990 CODE	**2007 CODE**
Canon 5D	Deleted
Applicability	
1990 CODE	**2007 CODE**
Canon 5E	Deleted
Application	Application

2007 CODE TO 1990 CODE

2007 CODE	1990 CODE
Preamble	Preamble (partial) and Canon 1A
Scope	Preamble (partial)
Terminology	Terminology
Application	Application
Canon 1	Canons 1 and 2
Compliance with the Law	
2007 CODE	1990 CODE
Rule 1.1	Canon 2A (partial)
Promoting Confidence in the Judiciary	
2007 CODE	1990 CODE
Rule 1.2	Canons 2 and 2A (partial)
Avoiding Abuse of the Prestige of Judicial Office	
2007 CODE	1990 CODE
Rule 1.3	Canon 2B (partial)
Performing the Duties of Judicial Office	
2007 CODE	1990 CODE
Canon 2	**Canon 3**
Giving Precedence to the Duties of Judicial Office	
2007 CODE	1990 CODE
Rule 2.1	Canon 3A
Impartiality and Fairness	
2007 CODE	1990 CODE
Rule 2.2	Canons 3B(2) (partial) and 3B(8)

Bias, Prejudice, and Harassment	
2007 CODE	**1990 CODE**
Rule 2.3(A)	Canon 3B(5) (partial)
Rule 2.3(B)	Canon 3B(5) (partial)
Rule 2.3(C)	Canon 3B(6) (partial)
Rule 2.3(D)	Canon 3B(6) (partial)

External Influences on Judicial Conduct	
2007 CODE	**1990 CODE**
Rule 2.4(A)	Canon 3B(2) (partial)
Rule 2.4(B)	Canon 2B (partial)
Rule 2.4(C)	Canon 2B (partial)

Competence, Diligence, and Cooperation	
2007 CODE	**1990 CODE**
Rule 2.5(A)	Canons 3B(2) (partial) and 3C(1) (partial) and 3B(8)
Rule 2.5(B)	3C(1) (partial)

Ensuring the Right to Be Heard	
2007 CODE	**1990 CODE**
Rule 2.6(A)	Canon 3B(7) (partial)
Rule 2.6(B)	Canon 3B(8) Commentary

Responsibility to Decide	
2007 CODE	**1990 CODE**
Rule 2.7	Canon 3B(1)

Decorum, Demeanor, and Communication with Jurors	
2007 CODE	**1990 CODE**
Rule 2.8(A)	Canon 3B(3)
Rule 2.8(B)	Canon 3B(4)
Rule 2.8(C)	Canon 3B(11)

Ex Parte Communication	
2007 Code	**1990 Code**
Rule 2.9(A)	Canon 3B(7) (partial)
Rule 2.9(A)(1)	Canon 3B(7)(a)
Rule 2.9(A)(1)(a)	Canon 3B(7)(a)(i)
Rule 2.9(A)(1)(b)	Canon 3B(7)(a)(ii)
Rule 2.9(A)(2)	Canon 3B(7)(b)
Rule 2.9(A)(3)	Canon 3B(7)(c)
Rule 2.9(A)(4)	Canon 3B(7)(d)
Rule 2.9(A)(5)	Canon 3B(7)(e)
Rule 2.9(B)	New
Rule 2.9(C)	Canon 3B(7) Commentary
Rule 2.9(D)	Canon 3B(7) Commentary
Judicial Statements on Pending and Impending Cases	
2007 Code	**1990 Code**
Rule 2.10(A)	Canon 3B(9) (partial)
Rule 2.10(B)	Canon 3B(10)
Rule 2.10(C)	Canon 3B(9)(partial)
Rule 2.10(D)	Canon 3B(9) (partial)
Rule 2.10(E)	New
Disqualification	
2007 Code	**1990 Code**
Rule 2.11(A)	Canon 3E(1)
Rule 2.11(A)(1)	Canon 3E(1)(a)
Rule 2.11(A)(2)	Canon 3E(1)(d)
Rule 2.11(A)(2)(a)	Canon 3E(1)(d)(i)
Rule 2.11(A)(2)(b)	Canon 3E(1)(d)(ii)
Rule 2.11(A)(2)(c)	Canon 3E(1)(d)(iii)
Rule 2.11(A)(2)(d)	Canon 3E(1)(d)(iv)
Rule 2.11(A)(3)	Canon 3E(1)(c)
Rule 2.11(A)(4)	Canon 3E(1)(e)
Rule 2.11(A)(5)	Canon 3E(1)(f)
Rule 2.11(A)(6)	Canon 3E(1)(b) (partial)

Disqualification (continued)	
2007 CODE	**1990 CODE**
Rule 2.11(A)(6)(a)	Canon 3E(1)(b) (partial)
Rule 2.11(A)(6)(b)	Canon 3E(1)(b) Commentary
Rule 2.11(A)(6)(c)	Canon 3E(1)(b) (partial)
Rule 2.11(A)(6)(d)	New
Rule 2.11(B)	Canon 3E(2)
Rule 2.11(C)	Canon 3F

Supervisory Duties	
2007 CODE	**1990 CODE**
Rule 2.12(A)	Canon 3C(2)
Rule 2.12(B)	Canon 3C(3)

Administrative Appointments	
2007 CODE	**1990 CODE**
Rule 2.13(A)	Canon 3C(4) (partial)
Rule 2.13(A)(1)	Canon 3C(4) (partial)
Rule 2.13(A)(2)	Canon 3C(4) (partial)
Rule 2.13(B)	Canon 3C(5)
Rule 2.13(B)(1)	Canon 3C(5)(a)
Rule 2.13(B)(2)	Canon 3C(5)(b)
Rule 2.13(B)(3)	Canon 3C(5)(c)
Rule 2.13(C)	Canon 3C(4) (partial)

Disability and Impairment	
2007 CODE	**1990 CODE**
Rule 2.14	New

Responding to Judicial and Lawyer Misconduct	
2007 CODE	**1990 CODE**
Rule 2.15(A)	Canon 3D(1) (partial)
Rule 2.15(B)	Canon 3D(2) (partial)
Rule 2.15(C)	Canon 3D(1) (partial)
Rule 2.15(D)	Canon 3D(2) (partial)

Cooperation with Disciplinary Authorities	
2007 CODE	**1990 CODE**
Rule 2.16(A)	New
Rule 2.16(B)	New

Personal and Extrajudicial Activities	
2007 CODE	**1990 CODE**
Canon 3	**Canon 4**

Extrajudicial Activities in General	
2007 CODE	**1990 CODE**
Rule 3.1	Canon 4A
Re 3.1(A)	Canon 4A(3)
Rule 3.1(B)	New (but derived from Canon 4(A)(3)
Rule 3.1(C)	Canon 4A(1)
Rule 3.1(D)	New
Rule 3.1(E)	Canon 2B (partial)

Appearances before Governmental Bodies and Consultation with Government Officials	
2007 CODE	**1990 CODE**
Rule 3.2	Canon 4C(1) (partial)
Rule 3.2(A)	Canon 4C(1) (partial)
Rule 3.2(B)	New
Rule 3.2(C)	Canon 4C(1) (partial)

Testifying as a Character Witness	
2007 CODE	**1990 CODE**
Rule 3.3	Canon 2B (partial)

Appointments to Governmental Positions	
2007 CODE	**1990 CODE**
Rule 3.4	Canon 4C(2)

Use of Nonpublic Information	
2007 CODE	**1990 CODE**
Rule 3.5	Canon 3B(12)

Affiliation with Discriminatory Organizations	
2007 CODE	**1990 CODE**
Rule 3.6(A)	Canon 2C
Rule 3.6(B)	Canon 2C Commentary

Participation in Educational, Religious, Charitable, Fraternal, or Civic Organizations and Activities	
2007 CODE	**1990 CODE**
Rule 3.7(A)	Canon 4C(3)
Rule 3.7(A)(1)	Canon 4C(3)(b)(i) (partial)
Rule 3.7(A)(2)	Canon 4C(3)(b)(i) (partial)
Rule 3.7(A)(3)	Canon 4C(3)(b)(iii)
Rule 3.7(A)(4)	New
Rule 3.7(A)(5)	Canon 4C(3)(b)(ii)
Rule 3.7(A)(6)	Canon 4C(3)(a)
Rule 3.7(A)(6)(a)	Canon 4C(3)(a)(i)
Rule 3.7(A)(6)(b)	Canon 4C(3)(a)(ii)
Rule 3.7(B)	New

Appointments to Fiduciary Positions	
2007 CODE	**1990 CODE**
Rule 3.8(A)	Canon 4E(1)
Rule 3.8(B)	Canon 4E(2)
Rule 3.8(C)	Canon 4E(3)
Rule 3.8(D)	Canon 4E Commentary

Service as Arbitrator or Mediator	
2007 CODE	**1990 CODE**
Rule 3.9	Canon 4F

Practice of Law	
2007 CODE	**1990 CODE**
Rule 3.10	Canon 4G

Financial, Business, or Remunerative Activities	
2007 CODE	1990 CODE
Rule 3.11(A)	Canon 4D(2)
Rule 3.11(B)	Canon 4D(3)
Rule 3.11(B)(1)	Canon 4D(3)(a)
Rule 3.11(B)(2)	Canon 4D(3)(b)
Rule 3.11(C)	Canon 4D(1)
Rule 3.11(C)(1)	Canon 4D(1) Commentary
Rule 3.11(C)(2)	Canon 4D(4)
Rule 3.11(C)(3)	Canon 4D(1)(b)
Rule 3.11(C)(4)	New

Compensation for Extrajudicial Activities	
2007 CODE	1990 CODE
Rule 3.12	Canons 4H(1) (partial) and 4H(1)(a)

Acceptance and Reporting of Gifts, Loans, Bequests, Benefits, or Other Things of Value	
2007 CODE	1990 CODE
Rule 3.13(A)	Canon 4D(5) (partial)
Rule 3.13(B)	Canon 4D(5) (partial)
Rule 3.13(B)(1)	Canon 4D(5)(h) (partial)
Rule 3.13(B)(2)	Canon 4D(5)(e)
Rule 3.13(B)(3)	Canon 4D(5)(c)
Rule 3.13(B)(4)	Canon 4D(5)(f)
Rule 3.13(B)(5)	New
Rule 3.13(B)(6)	Canon 4D(5)(g)
Rule 3.13(B)(7)	Canon 4D(5)(a) (partial)
Rule 3.13(B)(8)	Canon 4D(5)(b)
Rule 3.13(C)	Canon 4D(5) (partial)
Rule 3.13(C)(1)	Canon 4D(5)(a) (partial)
Rule 3.13(C)(2)	Canon 4D(5)(a) (partial)
Rule 3.13(C)(2)(a)	Canon 4D(5)(a) (partial)
Rule 3.13(C)(2)(b)	New
Rule 3.13(C)(3)	Canon 4D(5)(h)

Reimbursement of Expenses and Waivers of Fees or Charges	
2007 CODE	1990 CODE
Rule 3.14(A)	Canon 4H(1) (partial)
Rule 3.14(B)	Canon 4H(1)(b)
Rule 3.14(C)	Canon 4H(2)

Reporting Requirements	
2007 CODE	1990 CODE
Rule 3.15(A)	Canon 4H(2) (partial)
Rule 3.15(A)(1)	Canon 4H(2) (partial)
Rule 3.15(A)(2)	Canon 4H(2) (partial)
Rule 3.15(A)(3)	Canon 4H(2) (partial
Rule 3.15(B)	Canon 4H(2) (partial)
Rule 3.15(C)	Canon 4H(2) (partial)
Rule 3.15(D)	Canon 4H(2) (partial)

Political and Campaign Activity	
2007 CODE	1990 CODE
Canon 4	Canon 5

Political and Campaign Activities of Judges and Judicial Candidates in General	
2007 CODE	1990 CODE
Rule 4.1(A)	Canon 5A(1)
Rule 4.1(A)(1)	Canon 5A(1)(a)
Rule 4.1(A)(2)	Canon 5A(1)(c)
Rule 4.1(A)(3)	Canon 5A(1)(b)
Rule 4.1(A)(4)	Canon 5A(1)(e) (partial)
Rule 4.1(A)(5)	Canon 5A(1)(e) (partial)
Rule 4.1(A)(6)	New
Rule 4.1(A)(7)	New
Rule 4.1(A)(8)	Canon 5C(2) (partial)
Rule 4.1(A)(9)	Canon 5C(2) (partial)
Rule 4.1(A)(10)	New
Rule 4.1(A)(11)	Canon 5A(3)(d)(ii)
Rule 4.1(A)(12)	Canon 3B(9) (partial)
Rule 4.1(A)(13)	Canon 5A(3)(d) and (d)(i)
Rule 4.1(B)	Canon 5A(3)(b)

Political and Campaign Activities of Judicial Candidates in Public Elections	
2007 Code	**1990 Code**
Rule 4.2(A)	Canon 5C(1)
Rule 4.2(A)(1)	Canon 5A(3)(a)
Rule 4.2(A)(2)	New
Rule 4.2(A)(3)	New
Rule 4.2(A)(4)	Canon 5A(3)(c)
Rule 4.2(B)	Canon 5C(2) (partial)
Rule 4.2(B)(1)	Canon 5C(2) (partial)
Rule 4.2(B)(2)	Canons 5C(1)(b)(i) – (iii)
Rule 4.2(B)(3)	Canon 5C(1)(b)(iv)
Rule 4.2(B)(4)	Canon 5C(1)(a)(i)
Rule 4.2(B)(5)	New
Rule 4.2(B)(6)	Canon 5C(1)(a)(iii)
Rule 4.2(C)	Canon 5C(1)
Rule 4.2(C)(1)	Canon 5C(1)(a)(ii)
Rule 4.2(C)(2)	New
Activities of Candidates for Appointive Judicial Office	
2007 Code	**1990 Code**
Rule 4.3	Canon 5B
Rule 4.3(A)	Canon 5B(2)(a)(i)
Rule 4.3(B)	Canon 5B(2)(a)(ii)
Campaign Committees	
2007 Code	**1990 Code**
Rule 4.4(A)	Canon 5C(2) (partial)
Rule 4.4(B)	Canon 5C(2) (partial)
Rule 4.4(B)(1)	Canons 5C(2) (partial) and 5C(3)
Rule 4.4(B)(2)	Canon 5C(2) (partial)
Rule 4.4(B)(3)	Canon 5C(4)

Activities of Judges Who Become Candidates for Non-Judicial Office	
2007 CODE	**1990 CODE**
Rule 4.5(A) Rule 4.5(B)	Canon 5A(2) New (but implicit in and derived from Canon 5A(2))

APPENDIX B
REPORT TO THE HOUSE OF DELEGATES
REGARDING APPLICATION SECTION
(AUGUST 2010)

AMERICAN BAR ASSOCIATION

STANDING COMMITTEE ON ETHICS
AND PROFESSIONAL RESPONSIBILITY

REPORT TO THE HOUSE OF DELEGATES

RECOMMENDATION

APPLICATION

RESOLVED, That the American Bar Association amends the Application Section of the 2007 ABA Model Code of Judicial Conduct as follows (insertions **underlined in bold print**, deletions ~~struck through~~ **and in bold print**).

The Application section establishes when the various Rules apply to a judge or judicial candidate.

I.   APPLICABILITY OF THIS CODE
(A) The provisions of the Code apply to all full-time judges. Parts II through V of this section identify ~~those~~ provisions that apply to four ~~distinct~~ categories of part-time judges **only while they are serving as judges, and provisions that do not apply to part-time judges at any time. All other Rules are therefore applicable to part-time**

---

1. Each jurisdiction should consider the characteristics of particular positions within the administrative law judiciary in adopting, adapting, applying, and enforcing the Code for the administrative law judiciary. *See, e.g.,* Model Code of Judicial Conduct for Federal Administrative Law Judges (1989) and Model Code of Judicial Conduct for State Administrative Law Judges (1995). Both Model Codes are endorsed by the ABA National Conference of Administrative Law Judiciary.

judges at all times. The four categories of judicial service in other than a full-time capacity are necessarily defined in general terms because of the widely varying forms of judicial service. Canon 4 applies to judicial candidates.

(B) A judge, within the meaning of this Code, is anyone who is authorized to perform judicial functions, including an officer such as a justice of the peace, magistrate, court commissioner, special master, referee, or member of the administrative law judiciary.[1]

COMMENT

[1] The Rules in this Code have been formulated to address the ethical obligations of any person who serves a judicial function, and are premised upon the supposition that a uniform system of ethical principles should apply to all those authorized to perform judicial functions.

[2] The determination of which category and, accordingly, which specific Rules apply to an individual judicial officer, depends upon the facts of the particular judicial service.

[3] In recent years many jurisdictions have created what are often called "problem solving" courts, in which judges are authorized by court rules to act in nontraditional ways. For example, judges presiding in drug courts and monitoring the progress of participants in those courts' programs may be authorized and even encouraged to communicate directly with social workers, probation officers, and others outside the context of their usual judicial role as independent decision makers on issues of fact and law. When local rules specifically authorize conduct not otherwise permitted under these Rules, they take precedence over the provisions set forth in the Code. Nevertheless, judges serving on "problem solving" courts shall comply with this Code except to the extent local rules provide and permit otherwise.

II. RETIRED JUDGE SUBJECT TO RECALL

A retired judge subject to recall for service, who by law is not permitted to practice law, is not required to comply:

(A) with Rule 3.9 (Service as Arbitrator or Mediator), except while serving as a judge.; or

(B) at any time with Rule 3.8**(A)** (Appointments to Fiduciary Positions).

COMMENT

[1] For the purposes of this section, as long as a retired judge is subject to being recalled for service, the judge is considered to "perform judicial functions."

III. CONTINUING PART-TIME JUDGE

A judge who serves repeatedly on a part-time basis by election or under a continuing appointment, including a retired judge subject to recall who is permitted to practice law ("continuing part-time judge"),

(A) is not required to comply:
> (1) with Rule~~s 2.10(A), and 2.10(B))Judicial Statements on Pending and Impending Cases)~~ **4.1 (Political and Campaign Activities of Judges and Judicial Candidates in General) (A)(1) through (7)**, except while serving as a judge; or
> (2) at any time with Rules 3.4 (Appointments to Governmental Positions), 3.8**(A)** (Appointments to Fiduciary Positions), 3.9 (Service as Arbitrator or Mediator), 3.10 (Practice of Law), **and** 3.11**(B)** (Financial, Business, or Remunerative Activities) ~~3.14 Reimbursement of Expenses and Waivers of Fees or Charges, 3.15 (Reporting Requirements), 4.1 (Political and Campaign Activities of Judicial Candidates in Public Elections), 4.3 (Activities of Candidates for Appointive Judicial Office), 4.4 (Campaign Committees), and 4.5 (Activities of Judges Who Become Candidates for Nonjudicial Office)~~; and

(B) shall not practice law in the court on which the judge serves or in any court subject to the appellate jurisdiction of the court on which the judge serves, and shall not act as a lawyer in a proceeding in which the judge has served as a judge or in any other proceeding related thereto.

COMMENT

[1] When a person who has been a continuing part-time judge is no longer a continuing part-time judge, including a retired judge no longer subject

to recall, that person may act as a lawyer in a proceeding in which he or she has served as a judge or in any other proceeding related thereto only with the informed consent of all parties, and pursuant to any applicable Model Rules of Professional Conduct. An adopting jurisdiction should substitute a reference to its applicable rule.

IV. PERIODIC PART-TIME JUDGE

A periodic part-time judge who serves or expects to serve repeatedly on a part-time basis, but under a separate appointment for each limited period of service or for each matter,

(A) is not required to comply:

(1) with Rule 2.10 (Judicial Statements on Pending and Impending Cases and 4.1 (Political and Campaign Activities of Judges and Judicial Candidates in General) (A)(1) through (7), except while serving as a judge; or

(2) at any time with Rules 3.4 (Appointments to Governmental Positions), 3.7 (Participation in Educational, Religious, Charitable, Fraternal, or Civic Organizations and Activities; 3.8(A) (Appointments to Fiduciary Positions), 3.9 (Service as Arbitrator or Mediator), 3.10 (Practice of Law), and 3.11(B) (Financial, Business, or Remunerative Activities); 3.13 (Acceptance and Reporting of Gifts, Loans Bequests, Benefits, or Other Things of Value), 3.15 (Reporting Requirements), 4.1 (Political and Campaign Activities of Judges and Judicial Candidates in General), and 4.5 (Activities of Judges Who Become Candidates for Nonjudicial Office); and

(B) shall not practice law in the court on which the judge serves or in any court subject to the appellate jurisdiction of the court on which the judge serves, and shall not act as a lawyer in a proceeding in which the judge has served as a judge or in any other proceeding related thereto.

V. PRO TEMPORE PART-TIME JUDGE

A pro tempore part-time judge who serves or expects to serve once or only sporadically on a part-time basis under a separate appointment for each period of service or for each case heard is not required to comply:

78

(A) except while serving as a judge, with Rules ~~1.2 (Promoting Confidence in the Judiciary,~~ 2.4 (External Influences on Judicial Conduct), ~~2.10 (Judicial Statements on Pending and Impending Cases), or~~ 3.2 (Appearances before Governmental Bodies and Consultation with Government Officials), and **4.1 (Political and Campaign Activities of Judges and Judicial Candidates in General) (A)(1) through (7);** or

(B) at any time with Rules 3.4 (Appointments to Governmental Positions), ~~3.6 (Affiliation with Discriminatory Organizations), 3.7 (Participation in Educational, Religious, Charitable, Fraternal, or Civic Organizations and Activities),~~ 3.8**(A)** (Appointments to Fiduciary Positions), 3.9 (Service as Arbitrator or Mediator), 3.10 (Practice of Law), **and** 3.11**(B)** (Financial, Business, or Remunerative Activities), ~~3.13 (Acceptance and Reporting of Gifts, Loans Bequests, Benefits, or Other Things of Value), 3.15 (Reporting Requirements), 4.1 (Political and Campaign Activities of Judges and Judicial Candidates in General), and 4.5 (Activities of Judges Who Become Candidates for Nonjudicial Office)~~.

VI. Time for Compliance

A person to whom this Code becomes applicable shall comply immediately with its provisions, except that those judges to whom Rules 3.8 (Appointments to Fiduciary Positions) and 3.11 (Financial, Business, or Remunerative Activities) apply shall comply with those Rules as soon as reasonably possible, but in no event later than one year after the Code becomes applicable to the judge.

COMMENT

[1] If serving as a fiduciary when selected as judge, a new judge may, notwithstanding the prohibitions in Rule 3.8, continue to serve as fiduciary, but only for that period of time necessary to avoid serious adverse consequences to the beneficiaries of the fiduciary relationship and in no event longer than one year. Similarly, if engaged at the time of judicial selection in a business activity, a new judge may, notwithstanding the

prohibitions in Rule 3.11, continue in that activity for a reasonable period but in no event longer than one year.

FURTHER RESOLVED, that Comment [2] to Rule 2.10 of the Model Code of Judicial Conduct be amended to read as follows:

Rule 2.10: Judicial Statements on Pending and Impending Cases . . .
. . . .

COMMENT

[2] This Rule does not prohibit a judge from commenting on proceedings in which the judge is a litigant in a personal capacity**, or represents a client as permitted by these Rules**. In cases in which the judge is a litigant in an official capacity, such as a writ of mandamus, the judge must not comment publicly.

REPORT

At the February 2007 Midyear Meeting of the Association, on the recommendation of the ABA Joint Commission on Evaluation of the Model Code of Judicial Conduct and eight co-sponsoring entities, the ABA significantly revised the Model Code of Judicial Conduct.

In the period since February 2007, thirty-eight state jurisdictions have undertaken a review of the ABA's revisions to the Model Code of Judicial Conduct. As of January 2010, thirteen states have adopted revisions to their codes of judicial conduct based in whole or in part upon the ABA's action. Eight other states have recommendations pending for amendment of their judicial codes, and sixteen states are in the process of reviewing their codes.

This recommendation makes additional amendments to the Judicial Code relating to "part-time" judges. It serves both to strengthen the Judicial Code as an instrument expressing the Association's commitment to the administration of justice, and to facilitate its widespread and uniform adoption throughout the United States.

Several of the amendments were originally identified by state study committees during the course of their review of the 2007 Model Code. Others were identified by the Standing Committee on Ethics and Professional Responsibility in the course of its reexamination of the Application Section. In some instances, the amendments are intended to correct errors that occurred as the Judicial Code Evaluation Commission revised the provisions of the 1990 Judicial Code's Application Section to comply with the new organization and structure of the 2007 Judicial Code. In other instances, the Standing Committee identified situations in which the Application Section provisions were inconsistent with the 2007 Judicial Code's broad unifying principle: ensuring the independence, integrity, and impartiality of the judicial process among both full-time and part-time judges.

This recommendation draws upon valuable suggestions and comments from a variety of ABA entities representing the interests of all parties engaged in the judicial process, including judges, litigants, and their lawyers. It was guided throughout the process by the principle that, while the conduct of all judges, both full- and part-time, profoundly affects public perception of the judiciary's independence, impartiality, and integrity, the Code's provisions must be applied in recognition of judges' legitimate interests. Both the rule of reason and the particular circumstances surrounding judges' activities work in concert with the ABA Model Code of Judicial Conduct to provide guidance in this regard.

Explanation of the Function of the Application Section

Paragraph (A) of Section I of the Application Section describes the section as "identifying the provisions that apply to" part-time judges. A more precise statement of the function of the Section is that it *identifies specific provisions of the Code from which part-time judges are either sometimes, or always, exempt.* No substantive alteration of the Application Section is intended by the proposed language change.

Rule 1.2: Promoting Confidence in the Judiciary

One category among the various types of part-time judges—the "pro tempore part-time judge"—enjoys an exemption from the obligation imposed under Rule 1.2 to "act at all times in a manner that promotes public confidence in the independence, integrity, and impartiality of the judiciary, and . . .avoid impropriety and the appearance of impropriety." This Recommendation urges that because of their standing and recognition among the public, all judges should be obligated to uphold this standard. It therefore recommends that the existing exemption for "pro tempore part-time judges" be withdrawn.

Rule 2.10: Judicial Statements on Pending and Impending Cases

Among part-time judges, all but retired judges subject to recall are currently exempt, except while they are serving as judges, from the Rule 2.10 prohibition against making public statements that would impair the fairness of "a matter pending or impending in any court," or making "pledges, promises or commitments that are inconsistent with the impartial performance of the adjudicative duties of judicial office." There is no time at which a part-time judge, even if he or she is not presently serving, should be permitted to engage in these activities. This Recommendation therefore proposes, with respect to all four categories of part-time judge, the deletion of the exemption from compliance with Rule 2.10.

Note, however, that Comment [2] to Rule 2.10 should also be amended, to clarify that a judge (part-time or full-time) who is permitted to practice law does not violate Rule 2.10 by making appropriate public statements with respect to matters in which he or she represents a client as otherwise permitted under the Rules.

Rule 3.6: Affiliation with Discriminatory Organizations

Pro-tempore part-time judges, who are described in the Application Section as potentially having the most limited amount of service as judges, are currently exempt from Rule 3.6's prohibition against belonging to discriminatory organizations. It undermines the Model Code's pervasive commitment to the impartiality of the judiciary to permit any judges, no matter how infrequently they might serve, to belong to such organizations. This exemption in Section V. (B) should be deleted.

Rule 3.7: Participation in Educational, Religious, Charitable, Fraternal, or Civic Organizations and Activities

Periodic part-time judges and pro tempore part-time judges are both currently exempt from the provision of Rule 3.7 (C) that prohibits service on behalf of various types of organizations if such organizations "will be engaged in proceeding that would ordinarily come before the judge," or "proceedings in the court of which the judge is a member, or in any court subject to the appellate jurisdiction of the court of which the judge is a member." All part-time judges should be required to refrain from serving organizations of the type referred to in Rule 3.7 if those organizations' affairs would ordinarily come before them, and this Recommendation proposes to eliminate the exemptions contained in Sections IV. (B) and V. (B).

Rule 3.8: Appointments to Fiduciary Positions

All categories of part-time judges are currently exempt, at all times, from the restrictions of Rule 3.8. It does not serve the system properly— specifically with respect to ensuring the public's confidence of the impartiality of the courts—to permit part-time judges, at any time, to serve in a fiduciary capacity where they will be engaged in proceedings that would come before them, or any other member of the court on which they sit. Allowing such service invites two potential harms: requiring frequent disqualification of the part-time judge, and creating a potential for calling into question the impartiality of a judge hearing a matter in which a fellow judge is a participant. This Recommendation therefore proposes that the exemption from compliance with Rule 38 be modified to make paragraphs (B), (C), and (D) applicable to all categories of part- time judges. Paragraph (A), which is an across-the-board prohibition whose only exception is for services on behalf of family members, would continue to be inapplicable to part-time judges.

Rule 3.11: Financial, Business or Remunerative Activities

Among the four categories of part-time judges, all but the "Retired Judge Subject to Recall" are exempt, in Sections III, IV, and V of the Application Section, from the entirety of Rule 3.11. Although part-time judges frequently have a need, not experienced by full-time judges, to engage in various financial activities in order to support themselves and their families, such activities should nonetheless be limited to those that will not, as described in section (C) of Rule 3.11:

(1) interfere with the proper performance of judicial duties;
(2) lead to frequent disqualification of the judge;
(3) involve the judge in frequent transactions or continuing business relationships with lawyers or other persons likely to come before the court on which the judge serves; or
(4) result in violation of other provisions of this Code.

Consequently, this Recommendation provides that part-time judges in Sections III, IV, and V be subject to paragraph (C), but exempt from the broader prohibitions in paragraph (B).

Rule 3.13: Acceptance and Reporting of Gifts, Loans, Bequests, Benefits, or Other Things of Value

At present, only Retired Judges Subject to Recall and Continuing Part-time Judges are subject to the requirements of this Rule. This Recommendation provides that the exemption currently contained in Section IV (Periodic Part-time Judge) and Section V (Pro Tempore Part-time Judge) be deleted. No part-time judge ought to be allowed to violate Rule 3.13 (A)'s requirement that they not accept gifts or other things of value that would appear to a reasonable person to undermine the judge's independence, integrity, or impartiality. Neither should any part-time judge be allowed to accept—without reporting them under Rule 3.13(C)—gifts from parties or lawyers who come before them.

Rule 3.14: Reimbursement of Expenses and Waivers of Fees or Charges

Among the four categories of part-time judges, only the continuing part-time judge is exempt at present from the obligations or limitations imposed by Rule 3.14. If judges in the other categories, who can be presumed to have fewer potential conflicts in this regard, are compelled to comply with the Rule, the Rule should be applicable to continuing part-time judges as well.

Rule 3.15: Reporting Requirements

All part-time judges should be subject to the reporting requirements of Rule 3.15. It would be inconsistent for judges to be subject to Rules 3.12, 3.13, and 3.14, all of which include provisions that trigger public reporting, but not to be subject to the reporting requirement itself.

Rule 4.1: Political and Campaign Activities of Judges and Judicial Candidates in General

Rule 4.1 reorganizes and amalgamates under a single Rule various provisions taken from several of the 1990 Code's Canons. Some provisions from which judges should not be exempt have been erroneously combined with provisions from which judges do deserve to be exempt. The provisions of Rule 4.1A (1) through (7) all relate to conduct in which part-time judges deserve the opportunity to engage as long as they are not currently serving as judges, and this Recommendation amends Application Sections III, IV, and V to provide such an exemption. By contrast, all part-time judges should be prohibited from engaging in the conduct addressed in Rule 4.1(A)(8) through (13); no exemption from those provisions is provided.

Rule 4.2: Political and Campaign Activities of Judicial Candidates in Public Elections

Continuing part-time judges are at present exempt from compliance with Rule 4.2, whose requirements are established to ensure that the conduct of judges who are campaigning for judicial office—whether full-time or part-time office—will not undermine the independence, integrity, and impartiality of the judiciary. This Recommendation deletes the exemption for continuing part-time judges.

Rule 4.4: Campaign Committees

Section III of the Application Section exempts continuing part-time judges, who by description may serve by election, from the obligations imposed by Rule 4.4 to bear responsibility for the acts of members of their campaign committees. This obligation must be discharged by any judicial candidate, whether she be running for a full-time or part-time judgeship. Therefore, this Recommendation deletes the exemption now appearing in Section III.

Robert Mundheim, Chair
Standing Committee on Ethics and Professional Responsibility

August 2010

Appendix: Rules and Comment Subject to Proposed New Treatments in Application Section

RULE 1.2: Promoting Confidence in the Judiciary

A judge shall act at all times in a manner that promotes public confidence in the independence,* integrity,* and impartiality* of the judiciary, and shall avoid impropriety and the appearance of impropriety.

RULE 2.10: Judicial Statements on Pending and Impending Cases

(A) A judge shall not make any public statement that might reasonably be expected to affect the outcome or impair the fairness of a matter pending* or impending* in any court, or make any nonpublic statement that might substantially interfere with a fair trial or hearing.

(B) A judge shall not, in connection with cases, controversies, or issues that are likely to come before the court, make pledges, promises, or commitments that are inconsistent with the impartial* performance of the adjudicative duties of judicial office.

(C) A judge shall require court staff, court officials, and others subject to the judge's direction and control to refrain from making statements that the judge would be prohibited from making by paragraphs (A) and (B).

(D) Notwithstanding the restrictions in paragraph (A), a judge may make public statements in the course of official duties, may explain court procedures, and may comment on any proceeding in which the judge is a litigant in a personal capacity, or represents a client as permitted by these Rules.

(E) Subject to the requirements of paragraph (A), a judge may respond directly or through a third party to allegations in the media or elsewhere concerning the judge's conduct in a matter.

COMMENT

[1] This Rule's restrictions on judicial speech are essential to the maintenance of the independence, integrity, and impartiality of the judiciary.

[2] This Rule does not prohibit a judge from commenting on proceedings in which the judge is a litigant in a personal capacity. In cases in which the

judge is a litigant in an official capacity, such as a writ of mandamus, the judge must not comment publicly.

[3] Depending upon the circumstances, the judge should consider whether it may be preferable for a third party, rather than the judge, to respond or issue statements in connection with allegations concerning the judge's conduct in a matter.

RULE 3.6: Affiliation with Discriminatory Organizations

(A) A judge shall not hold membership in any organization that practices invidious discrimination on the basis of race, sex, gender, religion, national origin, ethnicity, or sexual orientation.

(B) A judge shall not use the benefits or facilities of an organization if the judge knows* or should know that the organization practices invidious discrimination on one or more of the bases identified in paragraph (A). A judge's attendance at an event in a facility of an organization that the judge is not permitted to join is not a violation of this Rule when the judge's attendance is an isolated event that could not reasonably be perceived as an endorsement of the organization's practices.

RULE 3.7: Participation in Educational, Religious, Charitable, Fraternal, or Civic Organizations and Activities

(A) Subject to the requirements of Rule 3.1, a judge may participate in activities sponsored by organizations or governmental entities concerned with the law, the legal system, or the administration of justice, and those sponsored by or on behalf of educational, religious, charitable, fraternal, or civic organizations not conducted for profit, including but not limited to the following activities:

(1) assisting such an organization or entity in planning related to fund-raising, and participating in the management and investment of the organization's or entity's funds;

(2) soliciting* contributions* for such an organization or entity, but only from members of the judge's family,* or from judges over whom the judge does not exercise supervisory or appellate authority;

(3) soliciting membership for such an organization or entity, even though the membership dues or fees generated may be used to support the objectives of the organization or entity, but only if the organization

or entity is concerned with the law, the legal system, or the administration of justice;

(4) appearing or speaking at, receiving an award or other recognition at, being featured on the program of, and permitting his or her title to be used in connection with an event of such an organization or entity, but if the event serves a fund-raising purpose, the judge may participate only if the event concerns the law, the legal system, or the administration of justice;

(5) making recommendations to such a public or private fund-granting organization or entity in connection with its programs and activities, but only if the organization or entity is concerned with the law, the legal system, or the administration of justice; and

(6) serving as an officer, director, trustee, or nonlegal advisor of such an organization or entity, unless it is likely that the organization or entity:

(a) will be engaged in proceedings that would ordinarily come before the judge; or

(b) will frequently be engaged in adversary proceedings in the court of which the judge is a member, or in any court subject to the appellate jurisdiction of the court of which the judge is a member.

(B) A judge may encourage lawyers to provide pro bono publico legal services.

RULE 3.8: Appointments to Fiduciary Positions

(A) A judge shall not accept appointment to serve in a fiduciary* position, such as executor, administrator, trustee, guardian, attorney in fact, or other personal representative, except for the estate, trust, or person of a member of the judge's family,* and then only if such service will not interfere with the proper performance of judicial duties.

(B) A judge shall not serve in a fiduciary position if the judge as fiduciary will likely be engaged in proceedings that would ordinarily come before the judge, or if the estate, trust, or ward becomes involved in adversary proceedings in the court on which the judge serves, or one under its appellate jurisdiction.

(C) A judge acting in a fiduciary capacity shall be subject to the same restrictions on engaging in financial activities that apply to a judge personally.

(D) If a person who is serving in a fiduciary position becomes a judge, he or she must comply with this Rule as soon as reasonably practicable, but in no event later than [one year] after becoming a judge.

RULE 3.11: Financial, Business, or Remunerative Activities

(A) A judge may hold and manage investments of the judge and members of the judge's family.*

(B) A judge shall not serve as an officer, director, manager, general partner, advisor, or employee of any business entity except that a judge may manage or participate in:

(1) a business closely held by the judge or members of the judge's family; or

(2) a business entity primarily engaged in investment of the financial resources of the judge or members of the judge's family.

(C) A judge shall not engage in financial activities permitted under paragraphs (A) and (B) if they will:

(1) interfere with the proper performance of judicial duties;

(2) lead to frequent disqualification of the judge;

(3) involve the judge in frequent transactions or continuing business relationships with lawyers or other persons likely to come before the court on which the judge serves; or

(4) result in violation of other provisions of this Code.

RULE 3.13: Acceptance and Reporting of Gifts, Loans, Bequests, Benefits, or Other Things of Value

(A) A judge shall not accept any gifts, loans, bequests, benefits, or other things of value, if acceptance is prohibited by law* or would appear to a reasonable person to undermine the judge's independence,* integrity,* or impartiality.*

(B) Unless otherwise prohibited by law, or by paragraph (A), a judge may accept the following without publicly reporting such acceptance:

(1) items with little intrinsic value, such as plaques, certificates, trophies, and greeting cards;

(2) gifts, loans, bequests, benefits, or other things of value from friends, relatives, or other persons, including lawyers, whose appearance or interest in a proceeding pending* or impending* before the judge would in any event require disqualification of the judge under Rule 2.11;

(3) ordinary social hospitality;

(4) commercial or financial opportunities and benefits, including special pricing and discounts, and loans from lending institutions in their regular course of business, if the same opportunities and benefits or loans are made available on the same terms to similarly situated persons who are not judges;

(5) rewards and prizes given to competitors or participants in random drawings, contests, or other events that are open to persons who are not judges;

(6) scholarships, fellowships, and similar benefits or awards, if they are available to similarly situated persons who are not judges, based upon the same terms and criteria;

(7) books, magazines, journals, audiovisual materials, and other resource materials supplied by publishers on a complimentary basis for official use; or

(8) gifts, awards, or benefits associated with the business, profession, or other separate activity of a spouse, a domestic partner,* or other family member of a judge residing in the judge's household,* but that incidentally benefit the judge.

(C) Unless otherwise prohibited by law or by paragraph (A), a judge may accept the following items, and must report such acceptance to the extent required by Rule 3.15:

(1) gifts incident to a public testimonial;

(2) invitations to the judge and the judge's spouse, domestic partner, or guest to attend without charge:

   (a) an event associated with a bar-related function or other activity relating to the law, the legal system, or the administration of justice; or

   (b) an event associated with any of the judge's educational, religious, charitable, fraternal or civic activities permitted by this Code, if the same invitation is offered to nonjudges who are engaged in similar ways in the activity as is the judge; and

(3) gifts, loans, bequests, benefits, or other things of value, if the source is a party or other person, including a lawyer, who has come or is

likely to come before the judge, or whose interests have come or are likely to come before the judge.

RULE 3.14: Reimbursement of Expenses and Waivers of Fees or Charges

(A) Unless otherwise prohibited by Rules 3.1 and 3.13(A) or other law,* a judge may accept reimbursement of necessary and reasonable expenses for travel, food, lodging, or other incidental expenses, or a waiver or partial waiver of fees or charges for registration, tuition, and similar items, from sources other than the judge's employing entity, if the expenses or charges are associated with the judge's participation in extrajudicial activities permitted by this Code.

(B) Reimbursement of expenses for necessary travel, food, lodging, or other incidental expenses shall be limited to the actual costs reasonably incurred by the judge and, when appropriate to the occasion, by the judge's spouse, domestic partner,* or guest.

(C) A judge who accepts reimbursement of expenses or waivers or partial waivers of fees or charges on behalf of the judge or the judge's spouse, domestic partner, or guest shall publicly report such acceptance as required by Rule 3.15.

RULE 3.15: Reporting Requirements

(A) A judge shall publicly report the amount or value of:

(1) compensation received for extrajudicial activities as permitted by Rule 3.12;

(2) gifts and other things of value as permitted by Rule 3.13(C), unless the value of such items, alone or in the aggregate with other items received from the same source in the same calendar year, does not exceed $[insert amount]; and

(3) reimbursement of expenses and waiver of fees or charges permitted by Rule 3.14(A), unless the amount of reimbursement or waiver, alone or in the aggregate with other reimbursements or waivers received from the same source in the same calendar year, does not exceed $[insert amount].

(B) When public reporting is required by paragraph (A), a judge shall report the date, place, and nature of the activity for which the judge received any compensation; the description of any gift, loan, bequest, benefit, or other thing of value accepted; and the source of reimbursement of expenses or waiver or partial waiver of fees or charges.

(C) The public report required by paragraph (A) shall be made at least annually, except that for reimbursement of expenses and waiver or partial waiver of fees or charges, the report shall be made within thirty days following the conclusion of the event or program.

(D) Reports made in compliance with this Rule shall be filed as public documents in the office of the clerk of the court on which the judge serves or other office designated by law,* and, when technically feasible, posted by the court or office personnel on the court's website.

RULE 4.2: Political and Campaign Activities of Judges and Judicial Candidates in General

(A) Except as permitted by law,* or by Rules 4.2, 4.3, and 4.4, a judge or a judicial candidate* shall not:

    (1) act as a leader in, or hold an office in, a political organization;*

    (2) make speeches on behalf of a political organization;

    (3) publicly endorse or oppose a candidate for any public office;

    (4) solicit funds for, pay an assessment to, or make a contribution* to a political organization or a candidate for public office;

    (5) attend or purchase tickets for dinners or other events sponsored by a political organization or a candidate for public office;

    (6) publicly identify himself or herself as a candidate of a political organization;

    (7) seek, accept, or use endorsements from a political organization;

    (8) personally solicit* or accept campaign contributions other than through a campaign committee authorized by Rule 4.4;

    (9) use or permit the use of campaign contributions for the private benefit of the judge, the candidate, or others;

    (10) use court staff, facilities, or other court resources in a campaign for judicial office;

    (11) knowingly,* or with reckless disregard for the truth, make any false or misleading statement;

    (12) make any statement that would reasonably be expected to affect the outcome or impair the fairness of a matter pending* or impending* in any court; or

(13) in connection with cases, controversies, or issues that are likely to come before the court, make pledges, promises, or commitments that are inconsistent with the impartial* performance of the adjudicative duties of judicial office.

(B) A judge or judicial candidate shall take reasonable measures to ensure that other persons do not undertake, on behalf of the judge or judicial candidate, any activities prohibited under paragraph (A).

RULE 4.2: Political and Campaign Activities of Judicial Candidates in Public Elections

(A) A judicial candidate* in a partisan, nonpartisan, or retention public election* shall:

(1) act at all times in a manner consistent with the independence,* integrity,* and impartiality* of the judiciary;

(2) comply with all applicable election, election campaign, and election campaign fund-raising laws and regulations of this jurisdiction;

(3) review and approve the content of all campaign statements and materials produced by the candidate or his or her campaign committee, as authorized by Rule 4.4, before their dissemination; and

(4) take reasonable measures to ensure that other persons do not undertake on behalf of the candidate activities, other than those described in Rule 4.4, that the candidate is prohibited from doing by Rule 4.1.

(B) A candidate for elective judicial office may, unless prohibited by law,* and not earlier than [insert amount of time] before the first applicable primary election, caucus, or general or retention election:

(1) establish a campaign committee pursuant to the provisions of Rule 4.4;

(2) speak on behalf of his or her candidacy through any medium, including but not limited to advertisements, websites, or other campaign literature;

(3) publicly endorse or oppose candidates for the same judicial office for which he or she is running;

(4) attend or purchase tickets for dinners or other events sponsored by a political organization* or a candidate for public office;

(5) seek, accept, or use endorsements from any person or organization other than a partisan political organization; and

(6) contribute to a political organization or candidate for public office, but not more than $[insert amount] to any one organization or candidate.

(C) A judicial candidate in a partisan public election may, unless prohibited by law, and not earlier than [insert amount of time] before the first applicable primary election, caucus, or general election:

(1) identify himself or herself as a candidate of a political organization; and

(2) seek, accept, and use endorsements of a political organization.

RULE 4.3: Activities of Candidates for Appointive Judicial Office

A candidate for appointment to judicial office may:

(A) communicate with the appointing or confirming authority, including any selection, screening, or nominating commission or similar agency; and

(B) seek endorsements for the appointment from any person or organization other than a partisan political organization.

RULE 4.4: Campaign Committees

(A) A judicial candidate* subject to public election* may establish a campaign committee to manage and conduct a campaign for the candidate, subject to the provisions of this Code. The candidate is responsible for ensuring that his or her campaign committee complies with applicable provisions of this Code and other applicable law.*

(B) A judicial candidate subject to public election shall direct his or her campaign committee:

(1) to solicit and accept only such campaign contributions* as are reasonable, in any event not to exceed, in the aggregate,* $[insert amount] from any individual or $[insert amount] from any entity or organization;

(2) not to solicit or accept contributions for a candidate's current campaign more than [insert amount of time] before the applicable primary election, caucus, or general or retention election, nor more than [insert number] days after the last election in which the candidate participated; and

(3) to comply with all applicable statutory requirements for disclosure and divestiture of campaign contributions, and to file with [name of appropriate regulatory authority] a report stating the name, address, occupation, and employer of each person who has made campaign contributions to the committee in an aggregate value exceeding $[insert amount]. The report must be filed within [insert number] days following an election, or within such other period as is provided by law.

RULE 4.5: Activities of Judges Who Become Candidates for Nonjudicial Office

(A) Upon becoming a candidate for a nonjudicial elective office, a judge shall resign from judicial office, unless permitted by law* to continue to hold judicial office.

(B) Upon becoming a candidate for a nonjudicial appointive office, a judge is not required to resign from judicial office, provided that the judge complies with the other provisions of this Code.

APPENDIX C
JUDICIAL ETHICS COMMITTEE

A. The [chief judge of the highest court of the jurisdiction] shall appoint a Judicial Ethics Committee consisting of [nine] members. [Five] members shall be judges; [two] members shall be non-judge lawyers; and [two] members shall be public members. Of the judicial members, one member shall be appointed from each of [the highest court, the intermediate levels of courts, and the trial courts.] The remaining judicial members shall be judges appointed from any of the above courts, but not from the [highest court of the jurisdiction]. The [chief judge] shall designate on of the members as chairperson. Members shall serve three-year terms; terms shall be staggered; and no individual shall serve for more than two consecutive terms.

B. The Judicial Ethics Committee so established shall have the authority to:

(1) by the concurrence of a majority of its members, express its opinion on proper judicial conduct with respect to the provisions of [the code of judicial conduct adopted by the jurisdiction and any other specified sections of law of the jurisdiction regarding the judiciary , such as financial reporting requirements], either on its own initiative, at the request of a judge or candidate for judicial office, or at the request of a court or an agency charged with the administration of judicial discipline in the jurisdiction, provided that an opinion may not be issued on a matter that is pending before a court or before such an agency except on request of the court or agency:

(2) make recommendations to [the highest court of the jurisdiction] for amendment of the Code of Judicial Conduct for the jurisdiction]; and

(3) adopt rules relating to the procedures to be used in expressing opinions, including rules to assure a timely response to inquiries.

C. A judge or candidate for judicial office as defined in the terminology Section of this Code who has requested and relied upon an opinion may not be disciplined for conduct conforming to that opinion.

D.   An opinion issues pursuant to this rule shall be filed with [appropriate official of the judicial conference of the jurisdiction]. Such an opinion is confidential and not public information unless [the highest court of the jurisdiction] otherwise directs. However, the [appropriate official of the judicial conference of the jurisdiction] shall caused an edited version of each opinion to be prepared, in which the identity and geographic location of the person who has requested the opinion, the specific court involved, and the identity of other individuals, organizations or groups mentioned in the opinion are not disclosed. Opinions so edited shall be published periodically in the manner [the appropriate official of the judicial conference of the jurisdiction] deems proper.

APPENDIX D
ABA STANDING COMMITTEE ON ETHICS AND PROFESSIONAL RESPONSIBILITY

COMPOSITION AND JURISDICTION

The Standing Committee on Ethics and Professional Responsibility, which consists of ten members, may:

(1) by the concurrence of a majority of its members, express its opinion on proper professional or judicial conduct, either on its own initiative or when requested to do so by a member of the bar or the judiciary;

(2) periodically publish its issued opinions to the profession in summary or complete form and, on request, provide copies of opinions to members of the bar, the judiciary and the public;

(3) provide under its supervision informal responses to ethics inquiries the answers to which are substantially governed by applicable ethical codes and existing written opinions;

(4) on request, advise or otherwise assist professional organizations and courts in their activities relating to the development, modification and interpretation of statements of the ethical standards of the profession such as the Model Rules of Professional Conduct, the predecessor Model Code of Professional Responsibility and the Model Code of Judicial Conduct;

(5) recommend amendments to or clarifications of the Model Rules of Professional Conduct or the Model Code of Judicial Conduct; and

(6) adopt rules relating to the procedures to be used in issuing opinions, effective when approved by the Board of Governors.

[The above Composition and Jurisdiction statement is found at 31.7 of the Bylaws of the Association. The Rules of Procedure are not incorporated into the Bylaws.]

RULES OF PROCEDURE

1. The Committee may express its opinion on questions of proper professional and judicial conduct. The Model Rules of Professional Conduct and the Model Code of Judicial Conduct, as they may be amended or superseded, contain the standards to be applied. For as long as a significant number of jurisdictions continue to base their professional standards on the predecessor Model Code of Professional Responsibility, the Committee will continue to refer also to the Model Code in its opinions.

2. The Committee may issue an opinion on its own initiative or upon a request from a member of the bar or the judiciary or from a professional organization or a court.

3. The Committee may issue opinions of two kinds: Formal Opinions and Informal Opinions. Formal Opinions are those upon subjects the Committee determines to be of widespread interest or unusual importance. Other opinions are Informal Opinions. The Committee will assign to each opinion a non-duplicative identifying number, with distinction between Formal Opinions and Informal Opinions.

4. The Committee will not usually issue an opinion on a question that is known to be pending before a court in a proceeding in which the requestor is involved. The Committee's published opinions will not identify the person who was the requestor or whose conduct is the subject of the opinion. The Committee will not issue an opinion on a question of law.

5. The Committee may invite or accept written information relevant to a particular opinion from a person or persons interested in such an opinion before the Committee begins its work on an opinion. Ordinarily, the Committee will not invite anyone to make an oral presentation or argument in support of that position.

6. When a Committee or staff member receives an inquiry about the status of a draft opinion from anyone outside the Committee, the member may inform the inquirer that the Committee is considering the question. Draft opinions may, in appropriate circumstances, be shown to other interested ABA Committees and entities. Committee and staff members shall not, absent unusual circumstances,

discuss the substance of pending opinions with the public, but may mention topics related to pending opinions in a general fashion.

7. Before issuing an opinion with respect to judicial conduct the Committee will submit the proposed opinion to the Judges Advisory Committee and consider any objection or comment from the Judges Advisory Committee and any member of it. The Committee may assume that the Judges Advisory Committee and its members have no objection or comment if none is received by the Committee within 30 days after the submission.

8. If the Committee decides not to issue a requested opinion the requestor will be promptly notified.

9. The Committee will issue an opinion only with the concurrence of six members in a vote taken at a meeting or in a telephone conference call. When a Committee member votes against a position declaring a Committee policy, that vote may be recorded in the minutes, which may include the name of the dissenting Committee member. The minutes shall not reflect the names of Committee members voting for or against any non-Committee policy question except that a member's vote shall be recorded and identified at the member's request. When drafting an opinion, policy statement or other document to be publicly disseminated, the Committee shall make every effort to reach a consensus. When, after a full examination of the issue and an exchange of views, the Committee cannot reach a consensus, a dissenting opinion may be appropriate to express the views of a Committee member or members. A member may place a statement of dissent in the Committee file or request that the dissent be published with the opinion.

10. The Chair may assign to one or more members the responsibility of preparing a proposed opinion for consideration by the Committee. The Committee will issue a requested opinion as promptly as feasible.

11. A Formal Opinion overrules an earlier Formal Opinion or Informal Opinion to the extent of conflict. An Informal Opinion overrules an earlier Informal Opinion to the extent of conflict but does not overrule an earlier Formal Opinion.

APPENDIX E
ABA STANDING COMMITTEE ON ETHICS AND PROFESSIONAL RESPONSIBILITY

Formal Opinion 07-449
August 9, 2007
Lawyer Concurrently Representing Judge and Litigant Before the Judge in Unrelated Matters

A lawyer who is asked to represent a client before a judge and is simultaneously representing that judge in an unrelated matter may, under Model Rule 1.7(b), undertake the representation only if he reasonably believes that he will be able to provide competent and diligent representation to both the litigant and the judge and they give their informed consent, confirmed in writing.

Pursuant to Model Code of Judicial Conduct Rule 2.11(A), the judge in such a situation must disqualify herself from the proceeding over which she is presiding if she maintains a bias or prejudice either in favor of or against her lawyer. This disqualification obligation also applies when it is another lawyer in her lawyer's firm who is representing a litigant before her. However, absent such a bias or prejudice for or against her lawyer, under Judicial Code Rule 2.11(C), the judge may continue to participate in the proceeding if the judge discloses on the record that she is being represented in the other matter by one of the lawyers, and the parties and their lawyers all consider such disclosure, out of the presence of the judge and court personnel, and unanimously agree to waive the judge's disqualification.

If a judge is obligated to make disclosures in compliance with Judicial Code Rule 2.11(C), refuses to do so, and insists upon presiding over the matter in question, the lawyer's obligation of confidentiality under Model Rule 1.6 ordinarily would prohibit his disclosing to his other client his representation of the judge without the judge's consent, rendering it impossible to obtain the client's consent to the dual representation, as required by Model Rule 1.7(b). The lawyer's continued representation of the judge in such a circumstance constitutes an affirmative act effectively assisting the judge in her violation of the Judicial Code, and thereby violates Model Rule 8.4(f). The lawyer (or another lawyer in the lawyer's firm), in that circumstance, is obligated to withdraw from the representation of the judge under Model Rule 1.16.

The duty of confidentiality that the lawyer owes to the judge as a client prohibits his disclosing the judge's violation of the Judicial Code to the appropriate disciplinary agency, as would otherwise be required under Model Rule 8.3.1.[1]

In this opinion, we address the obligations of a judge, and a lawyer representing that judge, when the lawyer (or another lawyer in his law firm[2]) simultaneously represents another client in a proceeding before that judge.

As a threshold matter, the Committee notes that when a lawyer considers simultaneously representing a judge in a proceeding and another client whose matter is being presided over by that judge, the lawyer must treat the judge as he would treat any other client. Thus, he must determine, under Rule 1.7(a)(2), if there is a "significant risk" that the representation of either client will be materially limited by his responsibilities to the other client. If so, the lawyer may proceed with the representation under Rule 1.7(b) only if the lawyer reasonably believes that he will be able to provide competent and diligent representation to each affected client, and each affected client gives informed consent, confirmed in writing.

We begin our analysis with a consideration of a judge's obligations under Model Code of Judicial Conduct Rule 2.11, which addresses judicial disqualification, although the judge's compliance or noncompliance with the various provisions of Judicial Code Rule 2.11 inevitably creates certain ethical obligations for her lawyer as well.[3]

---

1. This opinion is based on the MODEL CODE OF JUDICIAL CONDUCT as adopted by the ABA House of Delegates in February 2007 and on the ABA MODEL RULES OF PROF'L CONDUCT as amended by the ABA House of Delegates through February 2007.

2. MODEL RULE 1.10, "Imputation of Conflicts of Interest: General Rule," operates in the context of the subject matter of this opinion to disqualify other lawyers in the lawyer's firm when the lawyer would be disqualified under MODEL RULE 1.7, "Conflict of Interest: Current Clients." Moreover, MODEL RULE 5.1, "Responsibilities of Partners, Managers, and Supervisory Lawyers," requires that reasonable measures be in place within a law firm to identify such conflicts.

3. *See, e.g.,* N.Y. Adv. Comm. on Judicial Ethics Op. 05-143 (Jan. 26, 2006), *available at* http://www.nycourts.gov/ip/judicialethics/opinions/05-143.htm (recusal required where law firm, representing party before judge, was consulted by judge about pending investigation of complaint of unethical conduct). *See also* Ariz. Sup. Ct. Judicial Ethics Adv. Comm. Adv. Op. 92-11 (Sept. 9, 1992) (Potential Conflicts When Appearing Attorney Belongs to the Same Law Firm as Attorney Representing the Judge in an Unre-

Judicial Code Rule 2.11 gives rise to three possible scenarios. In the first, the judge has a bias or prejudice in favor of, or against, the lawyer who is representing her. In the second, the judge does not have such a bias or prejudice, but recognizes that a reasonable person might suspect such bias or prejudice, and submits the matter for consideration by the parties to the litigation in which her lawyer is appearing. In the third, the judge makes no disclosure of her representation by the lawyer, and does not disqualify herself.

1. Admission of Bias or Prejudice under Judicial Code Rule 2.11(A)
Judicial Code Rule 2.11(A) provides generally that "a judge shall disqualify himself or herself in a proceeding in which the judge's impartiality might reasonably be questioned . . . ." The first specifically enumerated circumstance in which the question of a judge's impartiality may arise is found in Judicial Code Rule 2.11(A)(1), "[t]he judge has a personal bias or prejudice concerning a party or a party's lawyer . . . ." Although all other possible causes for disqualification are subject to possible waiver by the parties under Section (C) of Judicial Code Rule 2.11,[4] a judge's bias or prejudice for or against a lawyer makes disqualification mandatory, with no possibility of waiver (a significant change from the predecessor Model Code of Judicial Conduct). When a judge recognizes the existence of her bias or prejudice toward her lawyer and

---

lated Case), *available at* http://www.supreme.state.az.us/ ethics/ethics_opinions/92-11.pdf (judge who is represented by lawyer in lawsuit may preside over unrelated case in which member of lawyer's firm represents one of the parties).

4. The Committee notes that the standard for judicial disqualification for federal judges, set forth in 28 U.S.C. 455(a), contains no provision for possible waiver equivalent to Judicial Code Rule 2.11(C), providing only that "[a]ny justice, judge or magistrate judge of the United States shall disqualify himself in any proceeding in which his impartiality might reasonably be questioned." *See* Texaco v. Chandler, 354 F.2d 655, 657 (10th Cir. 1965), *cert. denied*, 383 U.S. 936 (1966) (trial judge disqualified because litigant's counsel had recently represented the judge in defense of unrelated civil damages action against judge in course of his judicial activity); Rapp v. Van Dusen, 350 F.2d 806, 814 (3d Cir. 1965) (trial judge, although having no personal interest, was disqualified from further sitting because in earlier aspect of case, he allowed counsel for litigant to act as his counsel in response to mandamus petition for vacation of his order transferring case to another district); Smith v. Sikorsky Aircraft, 420 F. Supp. 661, 662 (C.D. Cal. 1976) (trial judge, although having no personal bias, disqualified himself because litigant's counsel had, in prior unrelated cases, represented judge in responding to two mandamus petitions; counsel also had represented judge personally).

disqualifies herself, her lawyer's potentially conflicting ethical obligations cease to exist.

2. Judge's Disclosure of the Lawyer's Representation under Judicial Code Rule 2.11(C)

The Committee does not assume that, whenever a judge finds herself presiding over a matter in which a lawyer for one of the parties is concurrently representing her in an unrelated matter, she inevitably develops a personal bias or prejudice for or against her lawyer, thus triggering the mandatory and nonwaivable disqualification under Judicial Code Rule 2.11(A)(1). The existence or nonexistence of such bias or prejudice depends on the facts of any particular situation. When a judge reasonably concludes that she is not personally biased or prejudiced toward her lawyer, she may continue to preside over the matter as long as she complies with the remaining requirements of Judicial Code Rule 2.11(C).

Judicial Code Rule 2.11(C) provides that a judge subject to possible disqualification under Judicial Code Rule 2.11(A) may continue to participate in the proceeding only if, as noted above, the disqualification does not involve the judge's personal bias or prejudice concerning a party or a party's lawyer.

In addition, the judge must disclose on the record the basis of her possible disqualification.[5] Thereafter, the parties and their lawyers must all consider, out of the presence of the judge and court personnel, whether to waive the disqualification and must unanimously agree that the judge should not be disqualified.

---

5. In ABA Standing Comm. on Ethics and Prof'l Responsibility Informal Op. 1477 (Aug. 12, 1981) (Requirement of Judicial Recusal When a Litigant is Represented by Judge's Lawyers), in FORMAL AND INFORMAL ETHICS OPINIONS, *Formal Opinions* 316-348, *Informal Opinions* 1285-1495 (ABA 1985) at 404, we stated that, based upon interpretation of Canon 3(C) of the 1972 Judicial Code, a judge was required to disqualify herself if she was represented by a lawyer who simultaneously represented a client before her. That opinion suggested that "[o]nly in unusual circumstances would a judge's impartiality not be subject to reasonable question when a lawyer appearing before the judge in behalf of a client is at the same time representing the judge in litigation pending before another court. . . ." The opinion nevertheless acknowledged that where the judge's relationship to the lawyer was "immaterial" and she had only an "insubstantial financial interest," remittal of disqualification would be permissible. *Id.* at 405.

3. Failure of the Judge to Comply with Judicial Code Rule 2.11

Lawyer's Participation in Judge's Misconduct

Finally, we address the ethical obligations of the lawyer whose judicial client fails to comply with Judicial Code Rule 2.11, thereby engaging in judicial misconduct.

Rule 8.4(f) states that it is professional misconduct for a lawyer "knowingly [to] assist a judge or judicial officer in conduct that is a violation of applicable rules of judicial conduct or other law."[6] In our opinion, a lawyer's continued participation in a case presided over by a judge who is acting in violation of Judicial Code Rule 2.11 constitutes "assistance" of that misconduct in violation of Rule 8.4(f). The Model Rules elsewhere acknowledge that assistance of another's wrongdoing does not require that the lawyer take affirmative steps in furtherance of the wrongdoing; in certain circumstances, silence can amount to improper assistance.[7] Here, the lawyer's silence would allow the judge to continue her violation of the Judicial Code.

Reminding the Judge of Her Obligation under Judicial Code Rule 2.11

A lawyer who hopes to avoid being a participant in the judge's misconduct may choose to communicate with the judge regarding her failure to comply with Judicial Code Rule 2.11(A). Such a communication is not, in our opinion, an improper ex parte communication as discussed and prohibited by both the Judicial Code and the Model Rules of Professional Conduct.

Judicial Code Rule 2.9(A) provides that "[a] judge shall not initiate, permit, or consider ex parte communications, or consider other communications made to the judge outside the presence of the parties or their lawyers, concerning a pending or impending matter. . . ." One of the policies underlying the prohibition against ex parte contacts is the prevention of undue influence on a judge through a lawyer's discussion of a

---

6. The judge's failure to disqualify herself also might amount to violation of "other law" under Rule 8.4(f) if such disqualification were required by a statute.

7. *See* Rule 4.1(b), "Truthfulness in Statements to Others" ("In the course of representing a client a lawyer shall not knowingly fail to disclose a material fact to a third person when disclosure is necessary to avoid assisting a criminal or fraudulent act by a client, unless disclosure is prohibited by Rule 1.6.").

matter outside the presence of the other lawyers or parties. Where, as here, the communication does not extend to the merits of the matter in question,[8] such a communication is permissible under Judicial Code Rule 2.9(A).

The communication also is permissible from the lawyer's perspective. Model Rule 3.5 prohibits a lawyer from seeking "to influence a judge, juror, prospective juror or other official by means prohibited by law" or from communicating "ex parte with such a person during the proceeding unless authorized to do so by law or court order." We do not believe that an attempt to dissuade a judge from conducting a proceeding constitutes an ex parte conversation with the judge during the proceeding within the meaning of Rule 3.5.

Lawyer's Independent Disclosure of Representation of the Judge

If the judge fails to withdraw from the matter or make appropriate disclosure on the record after the conversation with her lawyer, then the question arises whether the lawyer can either disclose the representation himself, without the judge's consent, or continue in the representation without the judge making the disclosure in reliance on the fact that all the parties and their lawyers already know about the judge's representation by the lawyer or a lawyer in his firm.

Under Rule 1.6(a), the fact of the lawyer's representation of the judge (or of representation of the judge by another lawyer in his firm), although not generally protected by the attorney-client privilege, nevertheless is considered confidential information. The lawyer, therefore, cannot reveal such information unless the lawyer has the consent of the judge (unlikely if the judge herself is unwilling to reveal the information), or has authority to do so under one of the exceptions to Rule 1.6.

The Committee notes that, even if disclosure by the lawyer was permitted, the disclosure could not effectively cure the judge's misconduct because it would leave unaddressed the question of whether or not the judge maintains a disqualifying bias or prejudice toward the lawyer, and it would do nothing to facilitate the necessary consideration by all parties, whether or not they chose to waive disqualification. For the same reasons, the judge's misconduct cannot be cured by reliance on the fact

---

8. Indeed, if the lawyer wished to exert undue influence, it is hardly likely that he would seek the judge's withdrawal under the circumstances.

that all parties to the matter already might be aware of the lawyer's representation of the judge in another matter.

Lawyer's Obligation to Withdraw from Representation

Earlier in this opinion, the Committee focused its attention on the considerations that a single lawyer must take into account when asked to undertake first one, and then a second, representation. In that circumstance, the ultimate question the lawyer needs to answer is whether he can undertake, or must decline, the second of the representations.

At least two situations can exist when the two representations are running concurrently. The first occurs when a lawyer already represents the judge and discovers that a pending matter in which he has been representing another client is going to come before that judge. A second occurs when two different lawyers from the same firm have undertaken the two representations without each other's knowledge. In either of these situations, the question that arises is not one of declining a representation, but one of deciding whether to withdraw from one or both representations.[9]

Having established that a lawyer's continued participation in a matter from which the judge has refused to disqualify herself in violation of Judicial Code Rule 2.11 would violate Rule 8.4(f),[10] the Committee is of the opinion that Rule 1.16, which concerns withdrawal from representation, requires that the lawyer withdraw from at least one, and possibly both, representations.[11]

Where the two representations are running concurrently and the judge has failed to make disclosure of her representation by one of the firm's lawyers, the Committee believes that, at least presumptively, the representation begun later in time is the one from which withdrawal would be required. For example, if a lawyer representing a client before a judge

---

9. Lawyers who either represent judges or practice in law firms that represent judges would be well-advised to monitor the firm's client list so that the lawyer and his firm can either avoid problems or, at the very least, recognize them before they become acute. This vigilance includes keeping the firm's conflicts database up-to-date in the event a firm client might become a judge during the representation. *See also* last section of this opinion, "Steps to Avoid Conflicts and Prevent Misconduct."

10. *See* note 6 and accompanying text.

11. Rule 1.16(a)(1) provides that a lawyer "shall withdraw from the representation of a client if . . . the representation will result in violation of the rules of professional conduct or other law."

learns that another lawyer in his firm previously had undertaken representation of the judge, and the judge refuses to comply with Judicial Code Rule 2.11(A), Rule 1.16(a)(1) would seem to require the law firm's withdrawal from representing the newer client because it is that representation that results in an inevitable violation of Rule 8.4(f).[12] However, if a lawyer begins to represent a judge and learns that another lawyer in his firm already has been representing a client in a matter before that judge, Rule 1.16(a) might be read to require the law firm's withdrawal from representing the judge, because the commencement of that representation triggered the lawyer's violation of Rule 8.4(f).

The examination of a lawyer's obligations under Rule 1.16 may not be complete when he identifies the need to withdraw from one of the representations. Withdrawal from the second matter may be indicated as well. For example, when a lawyer withdraws from the representation of a judge who refused to recuse herself, the judge might develop a bias against him, or some other lawyer in his firm, that would render it difficult or impossible to provide effective representation to the client whose matter is before the judge.

Additionally, the lawyer representing the client before the judge would be prohibited from disclosing the facts underlying the judge's possible bias or prejudice, making it impossible for him to obtain the client's consent to the continuation of the representation in spite of the judge's bias.

Thus, the lawyer may conclude that the required or most prudent course of conduct is to withdraw from both representations.[13] In that

---

12. The other firm lawyer who represents the judge might consider a discretionary withdrawal under Rule 1.16(b)(4) or some other provision if the other lawyer called upon the judge to comply with Judicial Code Rule 2.11 and the judge insisted on continuing to preside over the new client's matter without complying with that rule.

13. Theoretically, a judge who refuses to comply with Judicial Code Rule 2.11(A) also may refuse to allow the lawyer's withdrawal. We think that such judicial intransigence is improbable. Although Rule 1.16(c) indicates that a lawyer "shall continue representation notwithstanding good cause for terminating the representation" if the lawyer is ordered to do so by a tribunal, a lawyer confronting such an extraordinary circumstance might consider seeking relief from another judge or court, including a request that the matter be placed under seal. As in the context of a lawyer's mandatory withdrawal based on a client's misconduct, the court may request an explanation for the withdrawal, while the lawyer may be bound to keep confidential the facts that would constitute such an explanation; the lawyer's statement that professional considerations require termination of the representation ordinarily should be accepted as sufficient. Rule 1.16 cmt. 3.

event, the lawyer would continue to be prohibited from disclosing any information protected by Rule 1.6(a), unless the judge consented to the disclosure.

Whether to Report Judge's Misconduct

We do not believe that in the circumstances presented here, a lawyer can report his own client, the judge, to a disciplinary authority. As we stated in Formal Op. 04-433, Rule 1.6 takes precedence over any duty to report a client to a disciplinary authority.[14] Nor do we believe that any of the exceptions for permissive disclosure under Rule 1.6(b) apply. The judge's failure to recuse never would, as a practical matter, result in death or substantial bodily harm.

It also is difficult to imagine any circumstance in which the judge's failure to recuse constituted a crime or fraud that would result in substantial financial injury to another, in furtherance of which the judge is using the lawyer's services. The lawyer may, of course, under Rule 1.6(b)(4), reveal the judge's confidential information to another lawyer from whom the lawyer is seeking counsel as to his ethical obligations.

Duration of Judge's Disqualification

Neither the Model Code of Judicial Conduct nor the Model Rules of Professional Conduct prescribe specific time periods, subsequent to a judge's disqualification, within which a lawyer ought not to appear before the judge on behalf of a client.[15] In the Committee's opinion, questions as to the appropriateness of a lawyer's returning to a judge's court must be decided under the more general consideration underlying Judicial Code Rule 2.11(A), namely, whether a reasonable person would believe, in light of the time that had elapsed, that the judge's fairness and impartiality could still be questioned.[16] Factors to be considered in mak-

---

14. ABA Formal Op. 04-433 (Aug. 25, 2004) (Obligation of a Lawyer to Report Professional Misconduct by a Lawyer Not Engaged in the Practice of Law), slip op. at 6-7.

15. The Committee notes that Judicial Code Rule 2.11(A)(4) recommends that jurisdictions adopt a specific time limit for the disqualification required when a judge has accepted a campaign contribution from a lawyer or the lawyer's firm. We also note that the Judicial Code is otherwise silent as to time limitations related to disqualification for all other reasons.

16. N.Y. Adv. Comm. on Judicial Ethics, Op. 05-143, *supra* note 3, stated that the judge's recusal obligation expires two years after the judge last consults the lawyer on

ing that assessment include whether the matter was consequential (for example, defending the judge in a judicial disciplinary proceeding or responding to allegations regarding the judge's integrity), whether the matter was relatively inconsequential (for example, a routine real estate transaction), the size of the fee paid to the lawyer by the judge, whether the representation was isolated or one of several instances in which the lawyer represented the judge, and whether the representation was in a matter that was highly confidential or highly publicized.

Steps to Avoid Conflicts and Prevent Misconduct

There are numerous steps that a lawyer might helpfully consider when considering whether to represent a judge in the various circumstances discussed in this opinion. He might avoid the ethical problems altogether by including in his engagement letters a provision that, in the event the lawyer or a lawyer from his firm appears before the judge during the representation, the judge will either disqualify herself entirely or make appropriate disclosures on the record as required under the Judicial Code. A lawyer also may consider obtaining an advance waiver of confidentiality in the engagement letter, along with a recommendation that the judge seek the advice of independent counsel before consenting to such a waiver.

---

the matter giving rise to the disqualification. The New York Committee cited N.Y. Ethics Op. 92-54 (June 8, 1992), *available at* http://www.nycourts.gov/ip/judicialethics/opinions/92-54.htm, which provides a list of relevant factors for the judge to consider to determine if disqualification is the proper course, including "the nature of the instant proceeding, the nature of the prior representation by the attorney, and its frequency and duration, the length of time since the last representation, the amount of work done for the judge by the attorney and the amount of the fee, whether the representation was routine or technical or involved the morality of the judge's conduct, whether there exists a social relationship between the judge and the judge's former attorney, and whether there are any special circumstances creating a likely appearance of impropriety."

Formal Opinion 462
February 21, 2013
Judge's Use of Electronic Social Networking Media

A judge may participate in electronic social networking, but as with all social relationships and contacts, a judge must comply with relevant provisions of the Code of Judicial Conduct and avoid any conduct that would undermine the judge's independence, integrity, or impartiality, or create an appearance of impropriety.[1]

In this opinion, the Committee discusses a judge's participation in electronic social networking. The Committee will use the term "electronic social media" ("ESM") to refer to internet-based electronic social networking sites that require an individual to affirmatively join and accept or reject connection with particular persons.[2]

Judges and Electronic Social Media

In recent years, new and relatively easy-to-use technology and software have been introduced that allow users to share information about themselves and to post information on others' social networking sites. Such technology, which has become an everyday part of worldwide culture, is frequently updated, and different forms undoubtedly will emerge.

Social interactions of all kinds, including ESM, can be beneficial to judges to prevent them from being thought of as isolated or out of touch. This opinion examines to what extent a judge's participation in ESM raises concerns under the Model Code of Judicial Conduct.

Upon assuming the bench, judges accept a duty to "respect and honor the judicial office as a public trust and strive to maintain and enhance confidence in the legal system."[3] Although judges are full-fledged members of their communities, nevertheless, they "should expect to be the subject of public scrutiny that might be viewed as burdensome if applied to other citizens. . . ."[4] All of a judge's social

---

1. This opinion is based on the ABA Model CODE OF JUDICIAL CONDUCT as amended by the ABA House of Delegates through August 2012. The laws, court rules, regulations, rules of professional and judicial conduct, and opinions promulgated in individual jurisdictions are controlling.
2. This opinion does not address other activities such as blogging, participation on discussion boards or listserves, and interactive gaming.
3. Model Code, Preamble [1].
4. Model Code Rule 1.2 cmt. 2.

contacts, however made and in whatever context, including ESM, are governed by the requirement that judges must at all times act in a manner "that promotes public confidence in the independence, integrity, and impartiality of the judiciary," and must "avoid impropriety and the appearance of impropriety."[5] This requires that the judge be sensitive to the appearance of relationships with others.

The Model Code requires judges to "maintain the dignity of judicial office at all times, and avoid both impropriety and the appearance of impropriety in their professional and personal lives."[6] Thus judges must be very thoughtful in their interactions with others, particularly when using ESM. Judges must assume that comments posted to an ESM site will not remain within the circle of the judge's connections. Comments, images, or profile information, some of which might prove embarrassing if publicly revealed, may be electronically transmitted without the judge's knowledge or permission to persons unknown to the judge or to other unintended recipients. Such dissemination has the potential to compromise or appear to compromise the independence, integrity, and impartiality of the judge, as well as to undermine public confidence in the judiciary.[7]

There are obvious differences between in-person and digital social interactions. In contrast to fluid, face-to-face conversation that usually remains among the participants, messages, videos, or photographs posted to ESM may be disseminated to thousands of people without the consent or knowledge of the original poster. Such data have long, perhaps permanent, digital lives such that statements may

---

5. Model Code Rule 1.2. *But see* Dahlia Lithwick and Graham Vyse, "Tweet Justice," SLATE (April 30, 2010), (describing how state judge circumvents ethical rules prohibiting ex parte communications between judges and lawyers by asking lawyers to "de-friend" her from their ESM page when they're trying cases before her; judge also used her ESM account to monitor status updates by lawyers who appeared before her), *article available at* http://www.slate.com/articles/news_and_politics/jurisprudence/2010/04/tweet_justice.html.

6. Model Code, Preamble [2].

7. *See* Model Code Rule 1.2 cmt. 3. *Cf.* New York Jud. Eth. Adv. Op. 08-176 (2009) (judge who uses ESM should exercise appropriate degree of discretion in how to use the social network and should stay abreast of features and new developments that may impact judicial duties). Regarding new ESM website developments, it should be noted that if judges do not log onto their ESM sites on a somewhat regular basis, they are at risk of not knowing the latest update in privacy settings or terms of service that affect how their personal information is shared. They can eliminate this risk by deactivating their

be recovered, circulated or printed years after being sent. In addition, relations over the internet may be more difficult to manage because, devoid of in-person visual or vocal cues, messages may be taken out of context, misinterpreted, or relayed incorrectly.[8]

A judge who participates in ESM should be mindful of relevant provisions of the Model Code. For example, while sharing comments, photographs, and other information, a judge must keep in mind the requirements of Rule 1.2 that call upon the judge to act in a manner that promotes public confidence in the judiciary, as previously discussed. The judge should not form relationships with persons or organizations that may violate Rule 2.4(C) by conveying an impression that these persons or organizations are in a position to influence the judge. A judge must also take care to avoid comments and interactions that may be interpreted as *ex parte* communications concerning pending or impending matters in violation of Rule 2.9(A), and avoid using any ESM site to obtain information regarding a matter before the judge in violation of Rule 2.9(C). Indeed, a judge should avoid comment about a pending or impending matter in any court to comply with Rule 2.10, and take care not to offer legal advice in violation of Rule 3.10.

There also may be disclosure or disqualification concerns regarding judges participating on ESM sites used by lawyers and others who may appear before the judge.[9] These concerns have been addressed in

---

8. Jeffrey Rosen, "The Web Means the End of Forgetting", N.Y. Times Magazine (July 21, 2010) *accessible at* http://www.nytimes.com/2010/07/25/magazine/25privacy-t2.html?pagewanted=all.

9. *See, e.g.,* California Judges Ass'n Judicial Ethics Comm. Op. 66 (2010) (judges may not include in social network lawyers who have case pending before judge); Florida Sup. Ct. Jud. Eth. Adv. Comm. Op. 2009-20 (2009) (judge may not include lawyers who may appear before judge in social network or permit such lawyers to add judge to their social network circle); Ethics Committee of the Ky. Jud. Formal Jud. Eth. Op. JE-119 (judges should be mindful of "whether on-line connections alone or in combination with other facts rise to the level of 'a close social relationship'" that should be disclosed and/or require recusal); Ohio Sup. Ct. Bd. of Comm'rs on Grievances and Discipline Op. 2010-7 (2010) (judge may have ESM relationship with lawyer who appears as counsel in case before judge as long as relationship comports with ethics rules); South Carolina Jud. Dep't Advisory Comm. on Standards of Jud. Conduct, Op. No. 17- 2009 (magistrate judge may have ESM relationship with lawyers as long as they do not discuss anything related to judge's judicial position). *See also* John Schwartz, "For Judges on Facebook,

judicial ethics advisory opinions in a number of states. The drafting committees have expressed a wide range of views as to whether a judge may "friend" lawyers and others who may appear before the judge, ranging from outright prohibition to permission with appropriate cautions.[10] A judge who has an ESM connection with a lawyer or party who has a pending or impending matter before the court must evaluate that ESM connection to determine whether the judge should disclose the relationship prior to, or at the initial appearance of the person before the court.[11] In this regard, context is significant.[12] Simple designation as an ESM connection does not, in and of itself, indicate the degree or intensity of a judge's relationship with a person.[13]

Because of the open and casual nature of ESM communication, a judge will seldom have an affirmative duty to disclose an ESM con-

---

Friendship Has Limits," N.Y. TIMES, Dec. 11, 2009, at A25. *Cf.* Florida Sup. Ct. Jud. Eth. Adv. Comm. Op. 2010-04 (2010) (judge's judicial assistant may add lawyers who may appear before judge to social networking site as long as the activity is conducted entirely independent of judge and without reference to judge or judge's office).

10. *See* discussion in Geyh, Alfini, Lubet and Shaman, JUDICIAL CONDUCT AND ETHICS (5th Edition, forthcoming), Section 10.05E.

11. California Judges Assn. Judicial Ethics Comm. Op. 66 (need for disclosure arises from peculiar nature of online social networking sites, where evidence of connection between lawyer and judge is widespread but nature of connection may not be readily apparent). *See also* New York Jud. Eth. Adv. Op. 08-176 (judge must consider whether any online connections, alone or in combination with other facts, rise to level of close social relationship requiring disclosure and/or recusal); Ohio Opinion 2010-7 (same).

12. Florida Sup. Ct. Jud. Eth. Adv. Comm. Op. 2010-06 (2010) (judge who is member of voluntary bar association not required to drop lawyers who are also members of that organization from organization's ESM site; members use the site to communicate among themselves about organization and other non-legal matters). *See also* Raymond McKoski, "Reestablishing Actual Impartiality as the Fundamental Value of Judicial Ethics: Lessons from 'Big Judge Davis'," 99 KY. L.J. 259, 291 (2010-11) (nineteenth century judge universally recognized as impartial despite off-bench alliances, especially with Abraham Lincoln); Schwartz, *supra* note 9 ("Judges do not drop out of society when they become judges. . . . The people who were their friends before they went on the bench remained their friends, and many of them were lawyers.") (quoting New York University Prof. Stephen Gillers).

13. *See* Ethics Committee of the Ky. Jud. Formal Jud. Eth. Op. JE-119 (2010) (designation as an ESM follower does not, in and of itself, indicate the degree or intensity of judge's relationship with the person).

nection. If that connection includes current and frequent communication, the judge must very carefully consider whether that connection must be disclosed. When a judge knows that a party, a witness, or a lawyer appearing before the judge has an ESM connection with the judge, the judge must be mindful that such connection may give rise to the level of social relationship or the perception of a relationship that requires disclosure or recusal.[14] The judge must remember that personal bias or prejudice concerning a party or lawyer is the sole basis for disqualification under Rule 2.11 that is not waivable by parties in a dispute being adjudicated by that judge. The judge should conduct the same analysis that must be made whenever matters before the court involve persons the judge knows or has a connection with professionally or personally.[15] A judge should disclose on the record information the judge believes the parties or their lawyers might reasonably consider relevant to a possible motion for disqualification even if the judge believes there is no basis for the disqualification.[16] For example, a judge may decide to disclose that the judge and a party, a party's lawyer or a witness have an ESM connection, but that the judge believes the connection has not resulted in a relationship requiring disqualification. However, nothing requires a judge to search all of the judge's ESM connections if a judge does not have specific knowledge of an ESM connection that rises to the level of an actual or perceived problematic relationship with any individual.

---

14. *See, e.g.*, New York Judicial Ethics Advisory Opinion 08-176, *supra* n. 8. *See also* Ashby Jones, "Why You Shouldn't Take It Hard If a Judge Rejects Your Friend Request," WALL ST. J. LAW BLOG (Dec. 9, 2009) ("'friending' may be more than say an exchange of business cards but it is well short of any true friendship"); Jennifer Ellis, "Should Judges Recuse Themselves Because of a Facebook Friendship?" (Nov. 2011) (state attorney general requested that judge reverse decision to suppress evidence and recuse himself because he and defendant were ESM, but not actual, friends), *available at* http://www.jlellis.net/blog/should-judges-recuse-themselves-because-of-a-facebook-friendship/.

15. *See* Jeremy M. Miller, "Judicial Recusal and Disqualification: The Need for a Per Se Rule on Friendship (Not Acquaintance)," 33 PEPPERDINE L. REV. 575, 578 (2012) ("Judges should not, and are not, expected to live isolated lives separate from all potential lawyers and litigants who may appear before them However, it is also axiomatic that justice, to be justice, must have the appearance of justice, and it appears unjust when the opposing side shares an intimate (but not necessarily sexual) relationship with the judge").

16. Rule 2.11 cmt. 5.

Judges' Use of Electronic Social Media in Election Campaigns

Canon 4 of the Model Code permits a judge or judicial candidate to, with certain enumerated exceptions, engage in political or campaign activity. Comment [1] to Rule 4.1 states that, although the Rule imposes "narrowly tailored restrictions" on judges' political activities, "to the greatest extent possible," judges and judicial candidates must "be free and appear to be free from political influence and political pressure."

Rule 4.1(A)(8) prohibits a judge from personally soliciting or accepting campaign contributions other than through a campaign committee authorized by Rule 4.4. The Code does not address or restrict a judge's or campaign committee's method of communication. In jurisdictions where judges are elected, ESM has become a campaign tool to raise campaign funds and to provide information about the candidate.[17] Websites and ESM promoting the candidacy of a judge or judicial candidate may be established and maintained by campaign committees to obtain public statements of support for the judge's campaign so long as these sites are not started or maintained by the judge or judicial candidate personally.[18]

Sitting judges and judicial candidates are expressly prohibited from "publicly endorsing or opposing a candidate for any public office."[19] Some ESM sites allow users to indicate approval by applying "like" labels to shared messages, photos, and other content. Judges should be aware that clicking such buttons on others' political campaign ESM sites could be perceived as a violation of judicial ethics rules that prohibit judges from publicly endorsing or opposing another candidate for any public office.[20] On the other hand, it is unlikely to raise an ethics issue for a judge if someone "likes" or becomes a "fan" of the judge through the judge's ESM political campaign site if the campaign

---

17. In a recent survey, for judges who stood for political election, 60.3% used social media sites. 2012 CCPIO New Media and Courts Survey: A Report of the New Media Committee of the Conference of Court Public Information Officers (July 31, 2012), *available at* http://ccpio.org/blog/2010/08/26/judges-and-courts-on-social-media-report- released-on-new-medias-impact-on-the-judiciary/.

18. Florida Sup. Ct. Jud. Eth. Adv. Comm. Op. 2010-28 (July 23, 2010).

19. Model Code Rule 4.1(A)(3).

20. *See* "Kansas judge causes stir with Facebook 'like'," The Associated Press, July 29, 2012, *available at* http://www.realclearpolitics.com/news/ap/politics/2012/Jul/29/kansas_judge_causes_stir_with_facebook_like_.html.

is not required to accept or reject a request in order for a name to appear on the campaign's page.

Judges may privately express their views on judicial or other candidates for political office, but must take appropriate steps to ensure that their views do not become public.[21] This may require managing privacy settings on ESM sites by restricting the circle of those having access to the judge's ESM page, limiting the ability of some connections to see others, limiting who can see the contact list, or blocking a connection altogether.

Conclusion

Judicious use of ESM can benefit judges in both their personal and professional lives. As their use of this technology increases, judges can take advantage of its utility and potential as a valuable tool for public outreach. When used with proper care, judges' use of ESM does not necessarily compromise their duties under the Model Code any more than use of traditional and less public forms of social connection such as U.S. Mail, telephone, email or texting.

---

21. *See* Nevada Comm'n on Jud. Disc. Op. JE98-006 (Oct. 20, 1998) ("In expressing his or her views about other candidates for judicial or other public office in letters or other recorded forms of communication, the judge should exercise reasonable caution and restraint to ensure that his private endorsement is not, in fact, used as a public endorsement.").

Formal Opinion 470
May 20, 2015
Judicial Encouragement of Pro Bono Service

A state supreme court judge may sign a letter printed on the judge's stationery that is duplicated and mailed by the unified state bar association directed to all lawyers licensed in the state encouraging those lawyers to meet their professional responsibility under Rule 6.1 of the Model Rules of Professional Conduct and provide pro bono legal services to persons in need and to contact the bar association for information about volunteer opportunities.

A unified state bar association has asked a state supreme court justice to sign a letter encouraging lawyers to meet their obligations under Model Rule 6.1, Voluntary Pro Bono Public Service, and provide pro bono legal services to persons in need.[1] The letter will suggest that the recipient contact the bar association for information about volunteer opportunities.

The letter will be sent by the bar association on the justice's stationery to every member of the unified bar. Staff for the unified bar will manage and pay for its printing and mailing. The envelope for each letter to members of the bar will be personalized to the extent it will have the name and address of the bar member, but the salutation of the letter will not be personalized. The bar association will not track whether there is an increase in pro bono participation, nor will it report back to the justice on the responses it receives to the letter.[2]

Encouraging Lawyers to Provide Pro Bono Legal Services

Since their adoption in August 1983, the ABA Model Rules of Professional Conduct have included Rule 6.1, Pro Bono Publico Service. Rule 6.1 explains that lawyers have a "professional responsibil-

---

1. A unified bar association requires all lawyers licensed in the jurisdiction to be members of the association. Thirty states, the District of Columbia, U.S. Virgin Islands, Puerto Rico, Guam, and the Northern Mariana Islands are unified bars.

2. This opinion does not address the situation in which a judge asks a specific lawyer to accept appointment for a specific case. For those matters, see ABA Model Code of Judicial Conduct Rules 1.3, 2.13, 2.4, 3.1(D) and ABA Model Rules of Professional Conduct Rule 6.2.

ity to provide legal services to those unable to pay."[3] The Rule provides that lawyers should aspire to give 50 hours of free or reduced-cost legal services a year.

Rule 6.1 is a strong statement of the ABA's position on the duties of the profession.[4] The ABA Standing Committee on Lawyers' Public Service Responsibility, in its 1993 Report to House of Delegates, explained that Rule 6.1 was a meaningful response to the crisis that exists in providing legal services to the poor.[5]

Rule 3.7 of the ABA Model Code of Judicial Conduct allows judges to participate in organizations concerned with the law, the legal system, or the administration of justice subject to the limitations of Rule 3.1. Rule 3.7(B) reads: "A judge may encourage lawyers to provide pro bono publico legal services."

Comment [5] to Rule 3.7 explains this provision noting permitted conduct:

> . . . a judge may promote broader access to justice by encouraging lawyers to participate in pro bono publico legal

---

3. MODEL RULES OF PROF'L CONDUCT R. 6.1.

4. MODEL RULES OF PROF'L CONDUCT R. 6.1, cmt. [1].

5. According to the Legal Services Corporation's most recent nationwide study of unmet legal needs, approximately 944,000 people who sought legal help from LSC-funded offices in 2009 were turned away because the offices lacked adequate resources to help. *See* Legal Services Corporation, *Documenting the Justice Gap in America: The Current Unmet Civil Legal Needs of Low-Income Americans* (2009), http://www.lsc.gov/sites/default/files/LSC/pdfs/documenting_the_justice_gap_in_america_2009.pdf. "This means that for every client served by an LSC-funded program, at least one eligible person seeking help" was turned away. *Id.* at p. 12. More recent data from a spring 2014 report from the State Bar of Michigan noted three new developments that further threaten the ability of low income people to secure adequate representation. First, the recession has "dramatically increased the number of people in poverty" in Michigan, bringing with it an increase in the number of home foreclosures. Second, "Legal Services Corporation funding was cut 4% for 2011 and 15% for 2012." In Michigan, the results have been devastating for LSC staff. The number of lawyers available was reduced by 26 and three paralegals and more than 15 support staffers were laid off. Two offices have closed. As a result, almost 7,000 fewer matters can be processed. Finally, LSC-funded "programs are projected to face an additional 10% in funding cuts . . ." As a result, even fewer clients will have their needs met. State Bar of Michigan and the Michigan's Legal Services Corporation Funded Providers, *Documenting the Justice Gap in Michigan* (updated Spring 2015), https://www. michbar.org/programs/atj/pdfs/JusticeGap.pdf.

services, if in doing so the judge does not employ coercion, or abuse the prestige of judicial office. Such encouragement may take many forms, including providing lists of available programs, training lawyers to do pro bono publico legal work, and participating in events recognizing lawyers who have done pro bono publico work.

Rule 3.7(B) recognizes the symbiosis between lawyers' duties to provide pro bono services under Rule 6.1 of the Rules of Professional Conduct and judges encouraging lawyers to meet the obligations of Rule 6.1. The Reporters' Notes to the Model Code of Judicial Conduct explain that Rule 3.7(B) was a new provision in the 2007 Code designed to encourage judges to "provide leadership in increasing *pro bono publico* lawyering."[6] Rule 3.7(B) also is consistent with a judge's duties under Rule 1.2 to ensure "public confidence in the independence, integrity, and impartiality of the judiciary . . ." and to "promote access to justice for all."[7]

The facts presented require the Committee to construe the meaning and scope of Rule 3.7(B). This is a matter of first impression for the ABA.

Construing Rule 3.7(B) begins with the text of the Rule[8] The Committee notes that Rule 3.7(B) is permissive; judges may encourage lawyers to provide pro bono services, but judges are not required to do so. ABA Model Code of Judicial Conduct, Scope, paragraph [2] notes, "Where the Rule contains a permissive term, such as 'may' or 'should' the conduct being addressed is committed to the personal and professional discretion of the judge or candidate in question, and no disciplinary action should be taken for action or inaction within the bounds of such discretion."

Rule 3.7(B) allows judges to "encourage" lawyers to provide pro bono legal services. Although not defined by the Code, the Merriam-Webster Dictionary defines encouragement as making some-

---

6. CHARLES E. GEYH & W. WILLIAM HODES, REPORTERS' NOTES TO THE MODEL CODE OF JUDICIAL CONDUCT 70 (2009).

7. MODEL CODE OF JUDICIAL CONDUCT R. 1.2, cmt. [4].

8. "The words of a governing text are of paramount concern, and what they convey, in their context, is what the text means." ANTONIN SCALIA & BRYAN A. GARNER, READING LAW: THE INTERPRETATION OF LEGAL TEXTS 56 (2012).

one more determined, hopeful, or confident; making something more appealing or more likely to happen; and making someone more likely to do something. Comment [5] to Rule 3.7 notes that judicial encouragement to lawyers "may take many forms, including providing lists of available programs, training lawyers to do pro bono publico legal work, and participating in events recognizing lawyers who have done pro bono publico work."[9]

The word "including" in Comment [5] means that the actions noted are not an exhaustive list of how a judge might encourage lawyers to provide pro bono, but are examples.[10] Therefore, a judge is not limited to the activities noted in Comment [5] when encouraging lawyers to perform pro bono services. Although signing a letter encouraging lawyers to perform pro bono services is not one of the specific activities listed as permissible in Comment [5], the Committee thinks the Rules do not prohibit a judge from sending the encouraging letter described in this opinion. A judge signing a letter encouraging lawyers to contact the bar association for information on pro bono activities – for a list of available pro bono programs – is consistent with the encouragement listed in Comment [5]. This finding is in accord with a number of ethics opinions from around the country.[11]

---

9. Comments to the Rules are designed to provide examples of permitted conduct. *See* MODEL CODE OF JUDICIAL CONDUCT, Scope ¶ [3]. When the ABA House of Delegates adopted the 2007 Model CODE OF JUDICIAL CONDUCT, the House also adopted the Comments to the Code.

10. SCALIA GARNER, *supra* note 8, at 132.

11. *See* Alabama Jud. Inquiry Comm'n Adv. Op. 04-847 (2004) (judge may send letter asking lawyers to participate in state bar operated pro bono program); Florida Sup. Ct. Jud. Ethics Adv. Op. 2010-13 (2010) (judge may send general solicitation letter to "Members of the Bar" asking lawyers to participate in The Florida Bar's One Campaign for pro bono legal service); Florida Sup. Ct. Jud. Ethics Adv. Op. 2012-26 (2012) (judge may ask a local bar association to host an event at which the judge will ask lawyers to provide pro bono legal services; however, judge must monitor tone and delivery of the request to ensure it is not coercive); Maryland Jud. Ethics Comm. Op. 1996-20 (1996) (judge may write personal letters to lawyers asking lawyers to provide *pro bono* services); Texas Comm. on Jud. Ethics Op. 258 (2000) (board of judges may send letter to lawyers asking lawyers to consider providing pro bono service hours to joint project of local legal service organizations). *See also* Alaska Comm'n on Jud. Conduct Adv. Op. 2004-01 (2004) (judge may not refer lawyers to a particular pro bono program); Kentucky Ethics Comm. of the Judiciary Op. JE-107 (2005) (while a generic letter to the bar is permissible, judge may not urge lawyers to volunteer with a specific pro bono organization). *But see* Michigan Stand. Comm. on Prof'l & Jud. Ethics

Rule 3.7(A)(2) Does Not Prohibit Signing a Letter Encouraging Pro Bono Service

Rule 3.7(A)(2) prohibits a judge from soliciting contributions on behalf of a non-profit organization or governmental entity from anyone other than a family member or another judge over whom the soliciting judge "does not exercise supervisory or appellate authority." Though the Terminology of the Model Code of Judicial Conduct defines "personally solicit" as "a direct request made by a judge or a judicial candidate for financial support or in-kind services, whether made by letter, telephone, or any other means of communication" and "contributions" as including "professional or volunteer services," the Committee concludes that the letter is not a solicitation of a contribution for the reasons stated below.[12] Rather, it is a letter encouraging lawyers to meet their professional responsibility to provide pro bono legal services pursuant to Model Rule of Professional Conduct 6.1.

Rule 3.7(A)(2) and (B) can and should be read harmoniously for three reasons. First, "The provisions of a text should be interpreted in a way that renders them compatible, not contradictory."[13] If encouraging lawyers to contact the bar association for a list of pro bono opportunities was solicitation of a contribution under Rule 3.7(A)(2), then Rule 3.7's Comment [5]—which allows judges to "provide lists of available programs"—would be contradictory to Rule 3.7(A)(2).

Second, a contradictory reading would be unreasonable. The Scope section of the Model Code of Judicial Conduct explains, "The Rules of the Model Code of Judicial Conduct are rules of reason that should be applied consistent with constitutional requirements, statutes, other court rules, and decisional law, and with due regard for all relevant circumstances."

Finally, more support for this harmonious reading of paragraphs (A)(2) and (B) can be found in the legislative history of the Model

---

Op. J-7 (1998) (judge may not solicit individual lawyer to perform pro bono); Nebraska Jud. Ethics Comm. Adv. Op. 02-3 (2002) (judge may not sign recruiting letter for bar association pro bono campaign).

12. Because the Committee concludes that the letter is not a solicitation as prohibited by Rule 3.7(A)(2), it need not address whether there is a difference between a direct solicitation and a general one or how the interpretation of the Florida rules regarding solicitation by the U.S. Supreme Court in Williams-Yulee v. Florida Bar, 135 S.Ct. 1656 (2015) might apply.

13. SCALIA GARNER, *supra* note 8, at 180.

Code. Before the amendments of 2007, the Model Code of Judicial Conduct had no provision specifically allowing judges to encourage lawyers to provide pro bono service. Judicial ethics scholars involved with the ABA Joint Commission to Evaluate the Model Code of Judicial Conduct explained the interplay of the paragraphs. In their report accompanying the revisions, the scholars noted that it was "assumed that participation in organizations that promote *pro bono publico* legal services would generally be permissible under rule 3.7(A)"; nevertheless paragraph (B) was adopted to address encouraging pro bono "whether or not conducted in connection with a particular organization or entity."[14]

Model Rule 3.1, Extrajudicial Activities in General

A judge's extrajudicial activities are also guided by Model Rule 3.1. "Thus, even with respect to activities that are explicitly permitted by Rule 3.7, a judge must always consider whether participating in such activities, would on a more basic level, violate Rule 3.1, such as by leading to frequent disqualification."[15]

Rule 3.1 notes that while judges may engage in extrajudicial activities, they shall not:

(A) participate in activities that will interfere with the proper performance of the judge's judicial duties;

(B) participate in activities that will lead to frequent disqualification of the judge;

(C) participate in activities that would appear to a reasonable person to undermine the judge's independence, integrity, or impartiality;

(D) engage in conduct that would appear to a reasonable person to be coercive; or

(E) make use of court premises, staff, stationery, equipment, or other resources, except for incidental use for activities that concern the law, the legal system, or the administration of justice, or unless such additional use is permitted by law.

---

14. ABA JOINT COMMISSION TO EVALUATE THE MODEL CODE OF JUDICIAL CONDUCT, REPORT 200, 119-120 (Feb. 2007), http://www.americanbar.org/content/dam/aba/directories/policy/2007_my_200.authcheckdam.pdf.

15. GEYH & HODES, *supra* note 6, at 68.

Interfering with the proper performance of judicial duties

Rule 3.1(A)'s prohibition regarding interference with the proper performance of judicial duties is based on Model Rule 2.1. Model Rule 2.1 explains that a judge must perform the duties of the office and that official duties take precedence over personal and extrajudicial activities. A judge taking time to sign a letter encouraging lawyers to perform pro bono is a de minimis activity that will not interfere with the proper performance of the judge's duties.

In fact Rule 1.2 proclaims one judicial duty is to "act at all times in a manner that promotes public confidence in the independence, integrity, and impartiality of the judiciary, and shall avoid impropriety and the appearance of impropriety." Comment [4] gives an example of such actions explaining, "Judges should . . . promote access to justice for all."

A justice who signs the letter described in this opinion encouraging lawyers to seek out pro bono opportunities by contacting the bar association is promoting access to justice for all, consistent with Comment [4] of Rule 1.2.

Activities that lead to frequent disqualifications

Model Rule 3.1(B) prohibits judges from participating in activities that lead to frequent disqualification. Model Rule 2.11 addresses when a judge must disqualify himself or herself from hearing a matter. The Rule explains, in part, that:

> A judge shall disqualify himself or herself in any proceeding in which the judge's impartiality might reasonably be questioned, including but not limited to the following circumstances:
>
> (1) The judge has a personal bias or prejudice concerning a party or a party's lawyer, or personal knowledge of facts that are in dispute in the proceeding.
>
> ***
>
The Model Code of Judicial Conduct defines impartiality as "an absence of bias or prejudice in favor of, or against, particular parties or classes of parties, as well as maintenance of an open mind in con-

sidering issues that may come before a judge."[16] A judge who signs a general appeal letter encouraging lawyers to perform pro bono service does not thereby demonstrate a bias or prejudice toward any particular pro bono organization, the people any organization serves, or the lawyers who undertake that work.[17]

Activities that undermine the judge's independence, integrity, or impartiality

Model Rule 3.1(C) mirrors the language of Model Rule 1.2. That reads, in part, "A judge shall act at all times in a manner that promotes public confidence in the independence, integrity, and impartiality of the judiciary. . ."

The Model Code of Judicial Conduct defines independence as "a judge's freedom from influence or controls" in the decision-making process.[18] A judge must make decisions "independent of inappropriate outside influences."[19] Issues of judicial independence often arise in cases in which a judge has become an advocate for one party in a proceeding.[20] A judge who signs a letter encouraging lawyers to seek out pro bono opportunities by contacting the bar association is not being influenced or controlled in the decision-making process. Instead, the judge is encouraging lawyers to comply with Model Rule of

---

16. MODEL CODE OF JUDICIAL CONDUCT, Terminology.

17. This question also has been addressed in at least two states. Both the Alaska Commission on Judicial Conduct and the Alabama Judicial Inquiry Commission noted with approval that general appeals to participate in pro bono service are permissible and do not raise disqualification issues. Alaska Comm'n on Jud. Conduct Op. 2004-01 (2004) & Alabama Jud. Inquiry Comm'n Adv. Op. 04- 847 (2004).

18. MODEL CODE OF JUDICIAL CONDUCT, Terminology.

19. ANNOTATED MODEL CODE OF JUDICIAL CONDUCT 38 (2d ed. 2010).

20. *See, e.g., In re* Frankel, Karp, No. 12-118, Arizona Comm'n on Jud. Conduct (2012) (two judges disciplined for filing amicus brief in appeal of cases they heard because such action "failed to promote public confidence that judges are to be neutral and impartial and not advocates for particular legal results"); *In re* Graham, No. 09-31, Georgia Jud. Qualifications Comm'n (2010) (judge reprimanded for calling into chambers FBI agents investigating drug case and attacking their credibility and character in matter not assigned to judge and holding a hearing in chambers regarding a matter not before the judge); Disc. Counsel v. Campbell, 931 N.E.2d 558 (Ohio 2010) (judge became a participant in two investigations when he encouraged police to follow up on an issue, questioned defendants, and reviewed a prosecutor's file).

Professional Conduct 6.1 and promoting access to justice for all under Model Code of Judicial Conduct Rule 1.2.

The Model Code of Judicial Conduct defines integrity as "probity, fairness, honesty, uprightness, and soundness of character."[21] Probity is defined as complete honesty. Cases in which judges have been disciplined for failure to be honest include matters in which a judge has lied on a resume, deceived medical professionals to gain access to prescription drugs, and lied about attending CLE.[22] Uprightness and sound character cases include patterns of judicial behavior that demonstrate disrespect for the office.[23] A judge who signs a letter encouraging lawyers to seek out pro bono opportunities by contacting the bar association is not behaving unfairly, dishonestly, or disrespectfully. Instead, the judge is encouraging lawyers to comply with Model Rule of Professional Conduct 6.1.

The Model Code of Judicial Conduct defines impartiality as "an absence of bias or prejudice in favor of, or against, particular parties or classes of parties, as well as maintenance of an open mind in considering issues that may come before a judge."[24] Impartiality concerns are addressed in the opinion's discussion of disqualification, *supra.*

Activities that a reasonable person would find coercive

Both Rule 3.1(D) and Comment [5] to Rule 3.7 prohibit a judge from employing coercion while engaged in extrajudicial activities. The caution contained in Rule 3.1(D) was added to the 2007 Model Code

---

21. MODEL CODE OF JUDICIAL CONDUCT, Terminology.

22. *See In re* DeForest, Nos. 12-266 &12-275, Ariz. Comm'n on Jud. Conduct (2012) (justice of the peace reprimanded for inflating experience and training in on-line biography and on resume); Disc. Counsel v. Ault, 852 N.E.2d 727 (Ohio 2006) (judge got doctors to overprescribe painkilling drugs for his use); *In re* Augustus, 626 S.E.2d 346 (S.C. 2006) (judge lied about attending continuing legal education).

23. *See, e.g., In re* Carpenter, 17 P.3d 91 (Ariz. 2001) (judge removed for 14 Code violations); *In re* Jefferson, 753 So.2d 181 (La. 2000) (judge removed for pattern of conduct, including exceeding contempt power and banning city prosecutor from courtroom and thereafter dismissing 41 criminal cases when no prosecutor was present to proceed); *In re* Seitz, 495 N.W.2d 559 (Mich. 1993) (judge removed for hostile attitude toward employees, abuse of contempt power and other acts); Miss. Comm'n on Jud. Performance v. Spencer, 725 So.2d 171 (Miss. 1998) (judge removed for continuing pattern of offensive sexual comments).

24. MODEL CODE OF JUDICIAL CONDUCT, Terminology.

of Judicial Conduct because the ABA Joint Commission to Evaluate the Model Code of Judicial Conduct heard testimony about judges coercing others into supporting extrajudicial activities supported by the judge. The Joint Commission noted that judges using coercion "can be a significant problem in small communities with only one judge or a small number of judges and a small number of lawyers who need to maintain good relations with the judiciary."[25] Although the Model Code of Judicial Conduct does not define coercion or coercive practices, to coerce generally means to make or to get someone to perform some action by using force or threats.[26]

Rule 3.1(D) uses a reasonable person standard to determine whether a judge's conduct is coercive. Comment [4] to Rule 3.1 explains that a judge should avoid actions that risk that "the person solicited would feel obligated to respond favorably . . ." The totality of the facts should be reviewed to determine whether a judge's actions appear coercive to a reasonable person.

In this opinion, a state supreme court justice has been asked to send a general letter, with no personal salutation, to every lawyer in the state encouraging all lawyers to meet their professional responsibility under Rule 6.1 and provide pro bono legal services to those in need. The letter encourages lawyers to contact the state bar for a list of agencies in need. No follow-up monitoring will be conducted by the state bar, the supreme court, or the justice to determine whether every lawyer in the state has provided pro bono services.

Under these facts, the Committee does not think such a letter would be coercive. The letter is not threatening and would not lead a reasonable person to feel obligated to perform pro bono services. Additionally, such a letter would not lead a reasonable person to believe that

---

25. ANNOTATED MODEL CODE OF JUDICIAL CONDUCT 331 (2d ed. 2010).

26. *See* N.M. Adv. Comm. on Code of Jud. Conduct Op. 13-05 (2013) (judge could not preside over a school district's hearing-like truancy proceeding in his courtroom wearing his robes at which the truant student, the student's parents, and school personnel would speak with the judge about the student's truancy. Judge had no jurisdiction to conduct the quasi-hearing and the extra- judicial activity was coercive regardless of beneficial purpose of the actions). CHARLES GARDNER GEYH ET AL., JUDICIAL CONDUCT AND ETHICS §9.04 [2] (5th ed. 2013) (While the specific prohibition on coercive conduct first appeared in the CODE OF JUDICIAL CONDUCT in 2007, the prohibition against using intimidation to convince a potential donor into making a contribution is one of the concerns at the heart of the prohibition against soliciting contributions for a charitable organization).

the lawyer who performs pro bono services is currying favor with the justice because no follow-up will be conducted. The justice will not have knowledge of any lawyer's response to the letter.

At the same time, the Committee can foresee facts under which a letter from a judge urging a lawyer to perform pro bono legal services could be viewed as coercive by a reasonable person. Therefore, factors that a judge should weigh before sending a letter encouraging lawyers to perform pro bono include:

- The number of lawyers who will receive the letter. In smaller jurisdictions or in limited- scope mailings that are targeted at lawyers who practice in a particular area of the law, a reasonable person might feel coerced into providing pro bono legal services.
- The number of judges serving the jurisdiction. Again, in smaller jurisdictions with a limited number or only one judge, a lawyer who receives a letter from the judge encouraging that lawyer to provide pro bono legal services could feel coerced into doing so.
- Whether the letter is a personalized correspondence or a general plea to the bar as a whole. A letter in which the recipient lawyer is identified by name in the salutation runs the risk of a reasonable person finding such a letter coercive.
- Whether there will be some kind of post-letter monitoring. A letter in which a judge encourages a lawyer to perform pro bono legal services and then explains that the lawyer's participation, or lack thereof, will be monitored runs the risk of a reasonable person finding such a letter coercive.
- The tone of the letter. A letter in which the justice speaks in aspirational and encouraging language will have a much different impact than a letter that features dictatorial, condescending language.

Incidental Use of Court Resources for Activities that Concern the Law, the Legal System, or the Administration of Justice

Rule 3.1 cautions judges that when they engage in extrajudicial activities they must not use court premises, staff, stationery, equipment or other resources unless permitted by law or such use is incidental and is "for activities that concern the law, the legal system, or the administration of justice." Applying this caution to the facts in this opinion, the Committee notes that the justice's leadership of the state court system could easily be seen as part of the justice's judicial responsibility, and thus writing the letter may not be extrajudicial activity. Even if the activity were deemed to be extrajudicial, no court resources will be used to duplicate or mail the letter and only one piece of the justice's stationery need be used to create the general letter that will be sent to all lawyers in the jurisdiction, which is incidental use.

Model Rule 1.3, Avoiding Abuse of the Prestige of Judicial Office

Abuse of the prestige of judicial office is addressed in Rule 3.7 Comment [5] as well as Model Rule 1.3. We will address them together.

Rule 1.3, Avoiding Abuse of the Prestige of Judicial Office, reads: "A judge shall not abuse the prestige of judicial office to advance the personal or economic interests of the judge or others, or allow others to do so." Before 2007, the Model Code of Judicial Conduct prohibited judges from "lending" the prestige of their office. The Reporters' Notes to the 2007 Code explain that the ABA Joint Commission to Evaluate the Model Code of Judicial Conduct believed the word "abuse" more accurately described the conduct Rule 1.3 sought to prohibit. The goal was to address conduct that exploited the prestige of the office in inappropriate ways.[27] In their report to the House of Delegates, the Commission wrote, "In the Commission's view, the term 'lend' created unnecessary confusion."[28] As a result, the word "lend" was deleted from the rule.

The Committee is of the view that a supreme court justice does not abuse the prestige of judicial office when the justice signs a letter on court stationery encouraging lawyers to meet their professional responsibilities under Rule 6.1 and directing lawyers to the bar association for a list of organizations in need of pro bono assistance.[29]

---

27. GEYH & HODES, *supra* note 6, at 22-23.

28. ABA JOINT COMMISSION TO EVALUATE THE MODEL CODE OF JUDICIAL CONDUCT, *supra* note 14, at 38.

29. *See* Kentucky Ethics Comm. of the Judiciary Op. JE-107 (2005) (when crafting a general letter urging lawyers to perform pro bono, judges should "simply exhort the goodness and desirability of pro bono work" to avoid using the prestige of office). *But see* Nebraska Jud. Ethics Comm. Op. 02-3 (2002) (using the prior standard of "lend the prestige of judicial office").

Model Rule 2.4 External Influences on Judicial Conduct

ABA Model Rule 2.4(C) reads: "A judge shall not convey or permit others to convey the impression that any person or organization is in a position to influence the judge." Comment [1] to Rule 2.4 explains, "Confidence in the judiciary is eroded if judicial decision making is perceived to be subject to inappropriate outside influences." A judge who signs a general appeal letter mentioning no specific organization's need, but instead encouraging lawyers to perform pro bono service and directing lawyers to contact the bar association for a list of pro bono service organizations does not convey the impression that the judge's decisions can be influenced by a pro bono service organization or a person connected to a pro bono service organization. This letter writing activity is completely different than having an ex parte communication with one litigant[30] to a matter or holding separate and specially scheduled evening bond hearings,[31] for which judges have been found to violate Rule 2.4(C). Nor does the judge's letter writing activity permit the bar association or any pro bono organization to convey the impression that it is in a position to influence the judge.

Conclusion

A state supreme court judge may sign a letter printed on the judge's stationery that is duplicated and mailed by the unified state bar association directed to all lawyers licensed in the state encouraging those lawyers to meet their professional responsibility under Rule 6.1 of the Model Rules of Professional Conduct and provide pro bono legal services to persons in need and to contact the bar association for information about volunteer opportunities.

---

30. Miss. Comm. on Jud. Performance v. Lewis, 913 So.2d 266 (Miss. 1994).
31. *In re* David, 645 S.E.2d 243 (S.C. 2007).

Formal Opinion 478
December 8, 2017
Independent Factual Research by Judges Via the Internet

Easy access to a vast amount of information available on the Internet exposes judges to potential ethical problems. Judges risk violating the Model Code of Judicial Conduct by searching the Internet for information related to participants or facts in a proceeding. Independent investigation of adjudicative facts generally is prohibited unless the information is properly subject to judicial notice. The restriction on independent investigation includes individuals subject to the judge's direction and control. [1]

I. Introduction

The Internet provides immediate access to an unprecedented amount of information. Internet searches offer a vast array of information on endless topics. Social media sites provide extensive information that users share about themselves and others. Information discovered on the Internet may be highly educational and as useful to judges as judicial seminars and books. But information gathered from an Internet search may not be accurate. It may be biased, unreliable, or false. And, whether truthful or not, information discovered by a judge via the Internet that does not qualify for judicial notice and is not disclosed to the parties is untested by the adversary process. [2]

To help the judiciary navigate the hazards of Internet research, this opinion reviews the ethical parameters under the ABA Model Code

---

1. This opinion is based on the ABA Model Code of Judicial Conduct as amended by the ABA House of Delegates through August 2010. The laws, court rules, regulations, rules of professional and judicial conduct, opinions promulgated in individual jurisdictions and the Code of Conduct for United States Judges may be controlling. In addition, standards for judicial notice are beyond the scope of this opinion and discussed throughout only in general terms.

2. As used in this opinion, the term "judge" refers to "anyone who is authorized to perform judicial functions, including an officer such as a justice of the peace, magistrate, court commissioner, special master, referee, or member of the administrative law judiciary." *See* MODEL CODE OF JUDICIAL CONDUCT, Application § I(B) (2011).

of Judicial Conduct for conducting on-line independent fact-finding not tested by the adversary system.[3]

II. The ABA Model Code Provisions

The Preamble to the ABA Model Code of Judicial Conduct emphasizes that "[T]he United States legal system is based upon the principle that an independent, impartial, and competent judiciary, composed of men and women of integrity, will interpret and apply the law that governs our society."[4] This system requires that judges' decisions be based upon evidence presented on the record or in open court, and available to all parties. Except for evidence properly subject to judicial notice, a defining feature of the judge's role in an adversarial system is that the judge will "consider only the evidence presented by the parties."[5] Judges must be careful not to undermine this hallmark principle of judicial impartiality, or substitute for the time-honored role of the neutral and detached magistrate someone who combines the roles of advocate, witness, and judge.

A. *Ex Parte* Communications

Canon 2 of the Model Code states that a judge shall perform all duties of judicial office impartially, competently, and diligently.[6] An independent and impartial judiciary ensures the right of litigants to a fair trial. Impartiality is essential for the proper discharge of the judicial function.

---

3. Fact gathering over the Internet may occur, for example, via (i) search engines like Google, Yahoo, Bing, Duck Duck Go and others, or (ii) electronic social media that is interactive like Facebook, Twitter, or Instagram. *See, e.g.,* ABA Comm. on Ethics & Prof'l Responsibility, Formal Op. 462 (2013), *Judge's Use of Electronic Social Networking Media* (" 'electronic social media' . . . refer[s] to internet-based electronic social networking sites that require an individual to affirmatively join and accept or reject connection with particular persons") (footnote omitted). This opinion covers all types of Internet searching. In addition, while the opinion addresses independent research by judges on the Internet, some of the principles that are discussed also apply to more traditional research resources.

4. MODEL CODE OF JUDICIAL CONDUCT, Preamble [1] (2011).

5. CHARLES G. GEYH & W. WILLIAM HODES, REPORTERS' NOTES TO THE MODEL CODE OF JUDICIAL CONDUCT 40 (2009).

6. MODEL CODE OF JUDICIAL CONDUCT, Canon 2, R. 2.2 (a judge shall "perform all duties of judicial office fairly and impartially"); Rule 2.5(A) ("a judge shall perform judicial and administrative duties, competently and diligently").

Improper *ex parte* or "one-sided" communications undermine the independence and impartiality of the judiciary. Such communications create the appearance of bias or partiality on the part of the judge and, therefore, are precluded under the Model Code.

Model Rule 2.9(A) bars *ex parte* communications except in limited circumstances.[7] It provides: "A judge shall not initiate, permit, or consider ex parte communications, or consider other communications made to the judge outside the presence of the parties or their lawyers, concerning a pending or impending matter."[8] The ban on *ex parte* communication ensures that the judge will review and make rulings based only on the facts and evidence presented in the case.

B. Independent Fact Research Precluded

The Model Code's rule on *ex parte* communication includes a provision that specifically addresses independent investigation of facts. Model Rule 2.9(C) states: "A judge shall not investigate facts in a matter independently, and shall consider only the evidence presented and any facts that may properly be judicially noticed." Comment [6] to Rule 2.9 clarifies that the "prohibition against a judge investigating the facts in a matter extends to information available in all mediums, including electronic." [9]

---

7. Certain *ex parte* communications are permitted. The Model Code permits *ex parte* communications where they are permitted by law, such as in a settlement conference or certain applications for temporary equitable relief, or to address scheduling or administrative issues, or where the parties consent to permit *ex parte* communication, such as in an *in camera* review. A judge may discuss the case with court personnel. Judges may consult among or with other judges, court staff, and law clerks, *see* MODEL CODE OF JUDICIAL CONDUCT R. 2.9(A)(1)-(5) (2011); *id.* at cmt. [5], but as noted below, judges may not have others conduct research that the judge may not conduct.

8. The Model Code of Judicial Conduct defines "impending matter" as "a matter that is imminent or expected to occur in the near future." MODEL CODE OF JUDICIAL CONDUCT, Terminology (2011) (references omitted). A "pending matter" is "a matter that has commenced. A matter continues to be pending through any appellate process until final disposition." *Id.* (references omitted).

9. Thirty-one states have adopted Model Rule 2.9(C) or language substantially similar in their judicial codes. There is no similar provision in the Code of Conduct for United States Judges. For a discussion of independent fact-finding by state and federal judges generally see Hon. David B. Saxe, *"Toxic" Judicial Research*, N.Y. ST. B.J. 36 (Sept. 2015); Elizabeth F. Thornburg, *The Curious Appellate Judge: Ethical Limits on Independent Research*, 28 REV. LITIG. 131 (2008). For

Importantly, Rule 2.9(C) does not preclude legal research. Rule 2.9(C) carefully proscribes independent research of "facts." Judges may conduct legal research beyond the cases and authorities cited or provided by counsel.[10]

Rule 2.9(C) of the Model Code was adopted in 2007 and represents a significant clarification of the independent investigation proscription in the Internet age. Prior to 2007, the Model Code stated the general rule against *ex parte* communications and identified certain exceptions. The 1990 Model Code addressed independent investigation in a brief comment: "A judge must not independently investigate facts in a case and must consider only the evidence presented."[11] The 2007 change, moving the proscription from a comment to the text of the rule, was explained as follows:

In the Commission's view . . . the judge's duty to consider only the evidence presented is a defining feature of the judge's role in an adversarial system and warrants explicit mention in the black letter Rules.[12]

C. Judicial Notice of Facts

Rule 2.9(C) of the Model Code permits a judge to consider facts "that may properly be judicially noticed. . . . [U]nlike most provisions of the Code of Judicial Conduct, Rule 2.9(C) incorporates a section of

---

a discussion of whether federal judges may conduct independent research for purposes of obtaining what they consider to be "background" information if the information does not form the basis for a decision see Rowe v. Gibson, 798 F.3d 622 (7th Cir. 2015). For state-by-state adoption of Rule 2.9(C) see ABA, *CPR Policy Implementation Committee: Comparison of ABA Model Judicial Code and State Variations, Rule 2.9: Ex Parte Communication* (2016), http://www.americanbar.org/content/dam/aba/administrative/professional_responsibility/2_9.authcheckdam.pdf (last visited Nov. 21, 2017).

10. CHARLES G. GEYH, JAMES J. ALFINI, STEVEN LUBET & JEFFREY M. SHAMAN, JUDICIAL CONDUCT AND ETHICS, §5.04 at 5-25 (5th ed. 2013) ("independent investigation of *the law* has always been permitted" (emphasis in original); judges are "experts on matters of law who are charged with the duty of declaring what the law is"); *see also id.* at 5-24 to 5-25 (further discussion of independent research by judges).

11. *See* MODEL CODE OF JUDICIAL CONDUCT, Canon 3B(7), cmt. (1990).

12. ANNOTATED MODEL CODE OF JUDICIAL CONDUCT, 194 (3d ed. 2016) (citing CHARLES G. GEYH & W. WILLIAM HODES, REPORTERS' NOTES TO THE MODEL CODE OF JUDICIAL CONDUCT, *supra* note 5).

the law extrinsic to the Code; specifically, the law relating to judicial notice."[13]

For purposes of this opinion, Fed. R. Evid. 201(b)(1) and (2) contain an appropriate standard; they permit judicial notice of facts which are "not subject to reasonable dispute" because the facts are "generally known within the trial court's territorial jurisdiction" or "can be accurately and readily determined from sources whose accuracy cannot reasonably be questioned."[14] Judicial notice is "founded on the assumption that certain factual determinations are not subject to reasonable dispute and thus may be appropriately resolved other than by the production of evidence before the trier of fact at trial."[15]

Fed. R. Evid. 201(a) governs judicial notice of "adjudicative facts," not "legislative facts."[16] As the 1972 Advisory Committee Note to Rule 201(a) explains, this "terminology was coined by Professor Kenneth Davis in his article *An Approach to Problems of Evidence in the Administrative Process*, 55 HARV. L. REV. 364, 404–407 (1942)." The Advisory Committee Note explains that "adjudicative facts" are those "which relate to the parties" or, more fully:

> When a court or an agency finds facts concerning the immediate parties—who did what, where, when, how, and with what motive or intent—the court or agency is performing an adjudicative function, and the facts are conveniently called adjudicative facts. . . . Stated in other terms, the adjudicative facts are those to which the law is applied in the process of adjudication. They are the facts that normally go to the jury in a jury

---

13. Minn. Bd. on Jud. Standards Advisory Op. 2016-2 (2016).

14. A judge should be familiar with the jurisdiction's authority on judicial notice. The rules and process, even the definition of judicial notice, vary from jurisdiction to jurisdiction. Many state evidence codes track the language of Federal Rule of Evidence 201. *See* CAL. EVID. CODE ANN. § 452; FLA. ST. ANN. § 90.202; ILL. R. EVID. 201; PA. R. EVID. 201; TEX. R. EVID. R. 201. For a discussion of various state standards for judicial notice see O'Quinn v. Hall, 77 S.W.3d 438 (Tex. App. 2003); People v. Davis, 357 N.E.2d 792 (Ill. 1976); *In re* Cervera, 16 P.3d 176 n. 3 (2001); Maradie v. Maradie, 680 So. 2d 538 (Fla. Dist. Ct. App. 1996); Kinley v. Bierly, 876 A.2d 419 (Pa. Super. Ct. 2005).

15. MICHAEL H. GRAHAM, HANDBOOK OF FEDERAL EVIDENCE § 201:1 (7th ed. 2015) [hereinafter "GRAHAM"].

16. *See Federal Rules of Evidence Rule 201: Judicial Notice of Adjudicative Facts*, CORNELL LEGAL INFORMATION INSTITUTE, https://www.law.cornell.edu/rules/fre/rule_201 (last visited Nov. 27, 2017).

case. They relate to the parties, their activities, their properties, their businesses.[17]

"Legislative facts," on the other hand, "do not usually concern the immediate parties but are general facts which help the tribunal decide questions of law and policy and discretion."[18] Research of legislative facts does not raise the same due process concerns as research of adjudicative facts.

Procedural protections generally are built into taking judicial notice. Federal Rule of Evidence 201(e) provides that a party is entitled to be heard, either before or after a court takes judicial notice of a fact. If the court takes judicial notice of adjudicative facts, "[o]n timely request, a party is entitled to be heard on the propriety of taking judicial notice and the nature of the fact to be noticed. If the court takes judicial notice before notifying a party, the party, on request, is still entitled to be heard."[19]

D. Judge's Duty to Supervise

Model Rule 2.9(D) requires that judges take steps to prevent court staff and officials from performing improper independent investigations. The Rule provides: "A judge shall make reasonable efforts, including providing appropriate supervision, to ensure that this Rule is not violated by court staff, court officials, and others subject to the judge's direction and control."[20]

---

17. KENNETH CULP DAVIS, 2 ADMINISTRATIVE LAW TREATISE 353 § 15.03 *Legislative and Adjudicative Facts* (West 1958).

18. Usery v. Tamiami Trail Tours, Inc., 531 F.2d 224, 245, n. 52 (5th Cir. 1976) (*quoting* Davis, *An Approach to Problems of Evidence in the Administrative Process*, 55 HARV. L. REV. 364, 402-416 (1942)).

19. FED. R. EVID. 201(e). *See also* Garner v. Louisiana, 368 U.S. 157, 173 (1961) (citation omitted) ("[U]nless an accused is informed at trial of the facts of which the court is taking judicial notice, not only does he not know upon what evidence he is being convicted, but, in addition, he is deprived of any opportunity to challenge the deductions drawn from such notice or to dispute the notoriety or truth of the facts allegedly relied upon. Moreover, there is no way by which an appellate court may review the facts and law of a case and intelligently decide whether the findings of the lower court are supported by the evidence where that evidence is unknown. Such an assumption would be a denial of due process.")

20. MODEL CODE OF JUDICIAL CONDUCT R. 2.9(D) (2011).

III. Guidelines for Independent Factual Research by Judges Via the Internet

When deciding whether to independently investigate facts on the Internet, the judge should consider:

1. Is additional information necessary to decide the case? If so, this type of information generally must be provided by counsel or the parties, or must be subject to proper judicial notice.
2. Is the purpose of the judge's inquiry to corroborate facts, discredit facts, or fill a factual gap in the record? If the facts are adjudicative, it is improper for a judge to do so.
3. Is the judge seeking general or educational information that is useful to provide the judge with a better understanding of a subject unrelated to a pending or impending case? If so, the inquiry is appropriate. Judges may use the Internet as they would other educational sources, like judicial seminars and books.
4. Is the judge seeking background information about a party or about the subject matter of a pending or impending case? If so, the information may represent adjudicative facts or legislative facts, depending on the circumstances. The key inquiry here is whether the information to be gathered is of factual consequence in determining the case. If it is, it must be subject to testing through the adversary process.

III. Hypotheticals

The following hypotheticals are offered to provide guidance in determining whether independent research is permissible under the Model Code of Judicial Conduct.

Hypothetical #1: In a proceeding before the judge in a case involving overtime pay, defendant's counsel explains that the plaintiff could not have worked more than 40 hours per week because defendant's restaurant is in an "industrial area" and only open for breaks and lunch during the work-week and not on weekends. The judge is familiar with the area and skeptical of counsel's claims. The judge checks websites like Yelp and Google Maps, which list the restaurant as being open from 7 am to 10 pm, seven days each week. Does this search violate Rule 2.9(C) of the Model Code of Judicial Conduct?

Analysis #1: This search violates Rule 2.9(C) of the Model Code of Judicial Conduct because the restaurant's hours of operation are key to whether the plaintiff could prevail on a claim of unpaid overtime. The judge should ask the parties and their counsel to provide admissible evidence as to the restaurant's hours of operation.

Hypothetical #2: The judicial district in which the judge is assigned has many environmental contamination cases involving allegations that toxic chemicals have been released and have contaminated soil and groundwater. The judge is unfamiliar with this area of environmental law. Before a case is assigned to the judge, the judge reads online background information including articles. Does this action violate Rule 2.9(C) of the Model Code of Judicial Conduct?

Analysis #2: Judges may educate themselves by independent research about general topics of interest, even on topics that may come before the judge. General background learning on the Internet may be analogized to attending judicial seminars or reading books, so long as there is reason to believe the source is reliable. Even general subject-area research is not permissible, however, if the judge is acquiring information to make an adjudicative decision of material fact.[21]

---

21. *See, e.g.*, Cal. Judges Ass'n Jud. Ethics Comm. Advisory Op. 68 (2013) (judge may research basic principles of medicine or other disciplines prior to being assigned a matter; judge may not investigate relevant facts that are germane to the case); Minn. Bd. on Jud. Standards Advisory Op. 2016-2 at 2 (2016) (a judge is permitted to investigate non-adjudicative facts, including research on the general subject areas of cases coming before the judge, without informing the parties); N.Y. Advisory Comm. on Jud. Eth. Op. 13-32 (2013) (a judge may "consult a disinterested expert on the law with respect to a legal issue that is not currently before the judge, and is not the subject of a pending or impending proceeding with identifiable parties"). *Cf.* Model Rule 2.9(A) ("a judge shall not initiate, permit, or consider *ex parte* communications, or consider other communications made to the judge outside the presence of the parties or their lawyers, concerning a pending or impending matter," except as permitted under the rules); Model Rule 2.9(A)(2) (exception permitting a judge to "obtain the written advice of a disinterested expert on the law applicable to a proceeding before the judge, if the judge gives advance notice to the parties of the person to be consulted and the subject matter of the advice to be solicited, and affords the parties a reasonable opportunity to object and respond to the notice and to the advice received").

Hypothetical #3: A social media-savvy lawyer just has been appointed to the bench. Before being appointed, this lawyer used social media to conduct extensive background research on potential jurors and opposing parties. The judge has been assigned to hear a complex, multi-party case involving lawyers from out of state. The judge wants to review the social media and websites of each of the parties and of the out-of-state lawyers to learn background information about the parties, to read the lawyers' writings, and to review a list of the lawyers' current and former clients. Does this action violate Rule 2.9(C) of the Model Code of Judicial Conduct?

Analysis #3: While the Model Code of Judicial Conduct does not prohibit a judge from personally participating in electronic social media ("ESM"),[22] a "judge must . . . avoid using any ESM site to obtain information regarding a matter before the judge in violation of Rule 2.9(C)."[23] On-line research to gather information about a juror or party in a pending or impending case is independent fact research that is prohibited by Model Rule 2.9(C).[24]

Gathering information about a lawyer is a closer question. The judge's information-gathering about a lawyer may be permissible if it is done merely to become familiar with counsel who appear before the court similar to how a judge may have, in the past reviewed a legal directory like Martindale Hubbell, or to determine whether the lawyer is authorized to practice in the jurisdiction. However, the judge's independent research about a lawyer is not permitted if it is done to affect the judge's weighing or considering adjudicative facts. If an otherwise permissible review results in a judge obtaining information about the existence or veracity of adjudicative facts in the matter, the judge should ask the parties to address the facts in the proceeding through evidentiary submissions.[25]

---

22. *See* ABA Comm. on Ethics & Prof'l Responsibility, Formal Op. 462 at 2 (2013).

23. *Id.*

24. A judge may perform independent research to determine if a lawyer is authorized to practice in the jurisdiction, however, as this is not an adjudicative fact.

25. Two examples should suffice to make the point. The California Judges Association Judicial Ethics Committee Opinion 68 (2013) explained that a judge may not independently examine a state bar website to determine whether a potential juror is a lawyer to satisfy the judge's concern about that potential juror's veracity in responding to a question at *voir dire*. Instead the judge should "raise

Hypothetical #4: A trial judge presiding over an owner's claim for insurance coverage heard testimony from competing experts about their investigation and opinions about the cause of a fire that destroyed plaintiff's property. While preparing findings of fact and conclusions of law the judge received summaries her law clerk created from journals and articles on the proper techniques and analysis for investigating fires of unknown origin. Does this action violate Rule 2.9(C) of the Model Code of Judicial Conduct?

Analysis #4: By searching the Internet for journals and articles on investigating fires, the law clerk engaged in an improper independent factual investigation. The method and extent of the expert's investigation is an issue in dispute, *i.e.,* an adjudicative fact. The respective experts' investigative methods related directly to the weight and credibility given to testimony concerning an adjudicative fact, and fall within the prohibition in Rule 2.9(C). The trial court, therefore, could not properly take judicial notice of these facts as being "not subject to reasonable dispute" because they are neither "generally known within the trial court's jurisdiction" nor can they be "accurately and readily determined from sources whose accuracy cannot reasonably be questioned." Fed. R. Evid. 201(b). If the summaries addressed material facts in dispute and the judge used the summaries to make findings of fact without allowing the parties to test the factual content of the summaries through evidentiary submissions, the judge violated Model Rule of Judicial Conduct 2.9(A) by considering *ex parte* information, and violated Rule 2.9(D) by failing to require that the law clerk act in a manner consistent with the judge's obligations under the Code.[26]

---

the concerns with counsel and ask them to engage in follow-up factual research with respect to this potential juror." In NYC Medical and Neurodiagnostic, P.C. v. Republic Western Insurance Co., 798 N.Y.S.2d 309 (Appellate Term 2nd and 11th Dist. 2004), the New York Appellate Term reversed the trial court's order denying the defendant insurer's motion to dismiss, in part because the trial judge conducted independent factual research on the Internet. The judge used the Internet to access websites, including the New York State Department of Insurance website, to investigate whether the defendant was licensed to do business in the state because the plaintiff did not provide adequate proof on this issue.

26. As noted previously, Model Rule 2.9(A) provides that "[a] judge shall not initiate, permit, or consider ex parte communications . . . ." Model Rule 2.9(D) provides, "A judge shall make reasonable efforts, including providing appropriate supervision, to ensure that this Rule is not violated by court staff, court officials, and others subject to the judge's direction and control."

Hypothetical #5: To render an accurate decision in a pending matter, a judge needs to know whether a party is or was the subject of other judicial proceedings. The judge searches the court's electronic files of the other cases and the facts of each case, including sealed information. The search reveals several other cases, some pending and some concluded and some within and some outside the judge's jurisdiction. Does the judge's search violate Rule 2.9(C) of the Model Code of Judicial Conduct?

Analysis #5: Model Rule 2.9(C) does not prohibit consideration of "facts that may properly be judicial noticed." For example, a judge may take judicial notice of a guilty plea entered before the judge in a previous case[27] and of other court records maintained by the clerk of the court in which the judge sits.[28] Court records can be judicially noticed for their factual existence, and the occurrence and timing of matters like hearings held and pleadings filed, but not for the truth of allegations or findings therein.[29] "[T]he law treats different portions of

---

Disqualification is an additional risk that may arise from independent research in a pending case. Model Rule 2.11(A)(1) states that a "judge shall disqualify" him or herself when the judge has "personal knowledge of facts that are in dispute in the proceeding." Knowledge is "actual knowledge of the fact in question. A person's knowledge may be inferred from circumstances." MODEL RULES OF PROF'L CONDUCT, Terminology (2017). A judge likely has "personal knowledge" of facts that the judge has independently researched and found reliable. *See also* ANNOTATED MODEL CODE OF JUDICIAL CONDUCT (2d ed. 2011) ("Independent investigations by a judge . . . may provide a judge with personal knowledge of disputed facts, which is a special ground for judicial disqualification") (citations omitted).

27. *See* People v. Davis, 357 N.E.2d 792, 793-94 (Ill. 1976) (judicial notice of a conviction based upon a guilty plea in the same court before the same judge "falls squarely within the judicially noticeable category of facts 'capable of immediate and accurate demonstration by resort to easily accessible sources of indisputable accuracy'").

28. Ill. Jud. Ethics Comm. Op. 2016-02 (2016) (at sentencing, court may access county court files to review convicted criminal defendant's criminal case history "so long as the established procedural safeguards for taking judicial notice are adhered to"); Minn. Bd. of Jud. Standards, Advisory Op. 2016-2 (2016) (judge hearing *ex parte* order for protection may, under certain circumstances, take judicial notice of facts in Minnesota State Court Information Service).

29. Professional Engineers v. Department of Transportation, 936 P.2d 473, 496 (Cal. S. Ct. 1997) (construing a state Constitution's civil service provision that was later superseded by constitutional amendment; Ardaiz, J. dissenting, "judicial notice of findings of fact does not mean that those findings of fact are true, but, rather, only means that those findings of fact were made") (citations omitted); Doyle v.

the files and records differently."[30] Standards of judicial notice require the judge to give notice and an opportunity to be heard either before or after taking judicial notice. Again, each judge should determine the law of judicial notice in the applicable jurisdiction.

Even when reviewing court records, however, a judge should be mindful of the following caution, from Illinois Judicial Ethics Opinion 2016-02:

> the particular judge's competence to navigate the computerized court records is essential . . . only facts which are 'not subject to reasonable dispute' are the proper subject of judicial notice. The judge must be confident that his or her review will lead to *accurate* information. For example, indexes of computerized court records are likely to contain individuals with the same name; is the inquiring judge capable of finding the appropriate records and accurately matching them to the party in question? Judges must be aware of their own skills and, more importantly, their limitations . . . .

Documents that are sealed may not be reviewed. That would be independent research disclosing information about a party to which both sides do not have access or even know exist. Reviewing sealed documents is improper under Rule 2.9(C) of the Model Code of Judicial Conduct.[31]

People, 343 P.3d 961, 963 (Colo. S. Ct. 2015) ("Because the resolution of a factual matter at issue in a prior judicial proceeding, unlike the occurrence of the legal proceeding or other court action itself, does not become an indisputable fact within the contemplation of CRE 201 merely as a result of being reflected in a court record, the trial court erred in taking judicial notice that the defendant failed to appear in court on a particular day"); *see also* GRAHAM, *supra* note 15 § 201:3 for a full discussion of judicial notice of court records.

30. Minn. Bd. of Jud. Standards Advisory Op. 2016-2 (2016) *citing In re Welfare of D.J.N.*, 568 N.W.2d 170, 175 (Minn. Ct. App. 1997).

31. Wash. Ethics Advisory Comm. Op. 13-07 (2013) ("a judicial officer in a juvenile matter may not *sua sponte* review public and/or sealed records [maintained by the courts] unless such review is authorized by law"; "[i]f a party to a proceeding requests the court to review [the records] but such review is not expressly allowed by law, then the court should allow the other party or parties to be heard").

IV. Conclusion

The Internet provides useful tools for discovering vast amounts of information. Searching reliable sources on the Internet may reveal information that educates, informs, and enlightens the judiciary, not unlike judicial seminars and printed materials.

Information properly subject to judicial notice is well within the judge's discretion to search and use according to the applicable law. On the other hand, adjudicative facts that are needed to determine an issue in a case, but which are not properly subject to judicial notice, may not be researched without violating Rule 2.9(C). Stated simply, a judge should not gather adjudicative facts from any source on the Internet unless the information is subject to proper judicial notice. Further, and within the guidelines set forth in this opinion, judges should not use the Internet for independent fact-gathering related to a pending or impending matter where the parties can easily be asked to research or provide the information. The same is true of the activities or characteristics of the litigants or other participants in the matter.

Formal Opinion 485
February 14, 2019
Judges Performing Same-Sex Marriages

A judge for whom performing marriages is a mandatory obligation of judicial office may not decline to perform marriages of same-sex couples. A judge for whom performing marriages is a discretionary judicial function may not decline to perform marriages of same-sex couples if the judge agrees to perform opposite-sex marriages. A judge's refusal to perform same-sex marriages while performing opposite-sex marriages calls into question the judge's integrity and impartiality and reflects bias and prejudice in violation of Rules 1.1, 2.2, 2.3(A), and 2.3(B) of the Model Code of Judicial Conduct. In a jurisdiction in which a judge is not obligated to perform marriages but has the discretion to do so, a judge may refuse to perform marriages for members of the public. A judge who declines to perform marriages for members of the public may still perform marriages for family and friends. If a judge chooses to perform marriages for family and friends, however, the judge may not decline to perform same-sex marriages for family and friends.

Introduction

The Committee has been asked whether a judge subject to the Model Code of Judicial Conduct[1] may perform marriages of opposite-sex couples but refuse to perform marriages for same-sex couples. The Committee concludes that such a refusal violates the Model Code. A judge for whom performing marriages is a discretionary function may, however, decline to perform any marriages for members of the public. A judge who declines to perform any marriages for members of the public may still perform marriages for family and friends. If a judge chooses to perform marriages for family and friends, though, the judge may not decline to perform same-sex marriages for family and friends.

Background

The laws of all fifty states and the District of Columbia authorize one or more categories of judicial officers to perform marriages. This

---

1. MODEL CODE OF JUDICIAL CONDUCT (2011) [hereinafter MODEL CODE].

opinion covers judges for whom performing marriages is either a mandatory obligation of judicial office or a discretionary function.[2] The conclusions stated here are based solely on the Model Code.

The Model Code

Canon I of the Model Code articulates the bedrock principle that "[a] judge shall uphold and promote the independence, integrity, and impartiality of the judiciary, and shall avoid impropriety and the appearance of impropriety."[3] Rule 1.1 provides that "[a] judge shall comply with the law, including the Code of Judicial Conduct."[4] Accordingly, a judge must "act at all times in a manner that promotes public confidence in the independence, integrity, and impartiality of the judiciary, and shall avoid impropriety and the appearance of impropriety."[5] The term "impartiality" as used in this context means "the absence of bias or prejudice in favor of, or against, particular parties or classes of parties."[6]

Canon II expresses another fundamental principle: "A judge shall perform the duties of judicial office impartially, competently, and diligently."[7] Although a judge's performance of a marriage typically is a discretionary function rather than a mandatory function, it is nonetheless a duty of judicial office within the meaning of the Model Code.[8]

---

2. A judge, within the meaning of [the Model] Code, is anyone who is authorized to perform judicial functions, including an officer such as a justice of the peace, magistrate, court commissioner, special master, referee, or member of the administrative law judiciary." *Id.* at Application I(B).

3. *Id.* at Canon I.

4. *Id.* at R. 1.1. The Model Code defines the term "law" to include constitutional provisions, court rules, decisional law, and statutes. *Id.* Terminology.

5. *Id.* at R. 1.2.

6. *Id.* at Terminology.

7. *Id.* at Canon II.

8. *See, e.g., In re* Day, 413 P.3d 907, 950 (Or. 2018) (concluding that the act of solemnizing marriages, once a judge has chosen to do so, qualifies as a judicial duty within the meaning of judicial ethics rules), *cert. denied*, 139 S. Ct. 324 (2018); Ariz. Sup. Ct., Judicial Ethics Advisory Comm. Op. 15-01, 2015 WL 1530659, at *1 (2015) ("Although the performance of a marriage by a judge is a 'discretionary function' rather than a mandatory function . . . it is based on statutory authority granted by the legislature. Because of this specific grant of authority . . . the performance of a marriage by a judicial officer is performance of a 'judicial duty' as contemplated by the Code [of Judicial Conduct]."); Sup. Ct. of Ohio, Bd. of Prof'l Conduct Adv. Op. 15-001, 2015 WL 4875137, at *1 (2015) ("When a judge performs a civil marriage ceremony . . . the judge is performing a judicial

Correspondingly, Model Rule 2.2 requires a judge to "uphold and apply the law" and to "perform all duties of judicial office fairly and impartially."[9] Although judges come to the bench with different backgrounds and personal views or philosophies, judges "must interpret and apply the law, without regard to whether the judge approves or disapproves of the law" or principle or rule in question.[10] Model Rule 2.3(A) mandates that judges perform the duties of judicial office without bias or prejudice.[11]

Most importantly for present purposes, Model Rule 2.3(B) prohibits a judge who is performing judicial duties from manifesting bias or prejudice based on people's sex, gender, sexual orientation, or marital status.[12] A judge who manifests such bias or prejudice threatens to undermine public confidence in the judiciary and to bring it into disrepute.[13] Indeed, because impartiality and unbiased decision-making and conduct are critical to our justice system and to the public's faith in the judiciary, the Model Code emphasizes in several places that judges must avoid even conduct that may be *perceived* as biased or prejudiced.[14]

State Judicial Ethics Opinions

Several states have analyzed judges' obligations to perform same-sex marriages. In a leading opinion, the Supreme Court of Ohio Board

---

duty and is thus required to follow the CODE OF JUDICIAL CONDUCT in the performance of that duty."); Wis. Sup. Ct., Judicial Conduct Advisory Comm. Op. No. 15-1, 2015 WL 5928528, at *2 (2015) (discussing judges' discretionary functions in connection with the performance of marriages); Elizabeth A. Flaherty, *Impartiality in Solemnizing Marriages*, JUDICIAL CONDUCT BD. OF PA. NEWSLETTER, Summer 2014, at 18, 25 ("When a judge chooses to conduct a wedding ceremony, s/he acts in an official judicial capacity, authorized by statute.").

9. MODEL CODE R. 2.2, *supra* note 1.

10. *Id.* at cmt. [2].

11. *Id.* at R. 2.3(A).

12. *See id.* at R. 2.3(B) (prohibiting bias, prejudice, or harassment "based upon attributes including but not limited to race, sex, gender, religion, national origin, ethnicity, disability, age, sexual orientation, marital status, socioeconomic status, or political affiliation").

13. *Id.* at cmt. [1].

14. *See, e.g., id.* at Preamble cmt. [2] ("Judges should maintain the dignity of judicial office at all times, and avoid both impropriety and the *appearance of impropriety* in their professional and personal lives.") (emphasis added); *Id.* at R. 1.2 cmt. [3] ("Conduct that compromises or *appears to compromise the independence, integrity, and impartiality of a judge* undermines public confidence in the judiciary. . . . (emphasis added)).

of Professional Conduct was asked by judges and a judicial association on behalf of its members (1) whether a judge who is authorized to perform marriages may refuse to marry same-sex couples on personal, moral, or religious grounds, but still marry opposite-sex couples; and (2) whether a judge may decline to perform all marriages to avoid marrying same-sex couples.[15] Relying on the oath of office to which all Ohio judges swear, and provisions of the Ohio Code of Judicial Conduct, which track the Model Code, the Board concluded that "[a] judge who performs civil marriages may not refuse to perform same-sex marriages while continuing to perform opposite-sex marriages, based upon his or her personal, moral, and religious beliefs."[16] The Board further concluded that "[a] judge who takes the position that he or she will discontinue performing all marriages in order to avoid marrying same-sex couples based on his or her personal, moral, or religious beliefs may be interpreted as manifesting an improper bias or prejudice toward a particular class."[17] Thus, Ohio judges may not decline to perform all marriages to avoid marrying same-sex couples on personal, moral, or religious grounds.[18] Other authorities have disagreed on this final point, however, and have held that judges may decline to perform all marriages without manifesting bias or prejudice toward same-sex couples.[19]

The Arizona Supreme Court Judicial Ethics Advisory Committee concluded that judges may not (1) distinguish between same-sex and opposite-sex couples when deciding whether to perform marriage ceremonies; (2) decline to perform same-sex marriage ceremonies even if the judge refers would-be spouses to other courts or individuals; (3) decline to perform same-sex marriages if they perform other marriages in court facilities; or (4) decline to perform same-sex marriages even if they conduct all opposite-sex weddings

---

15. Sup. Ct. of Ohio, Bd. of Prof'l Conduct Advisory Op. 15-001, 2015 WL 4875137, at *1 (2015).

16. *Id.* at *5.

17. *Id.*

18. *Id.* at *1, *5.

19. *See, e.g.,* Wis. Sup. Ct., Judicial Conduct Advisory Comm. Op. 15-1, 2015 WL 5928528, at *1 (2015) (stating that judicial officers may not decline to officiate at same-sex weddings because of their religious or personal beliefs, but that judicial officers may decline to perform marriages at all, regardless of whether the parties seeking to be married are of the same or opposite genders, because officiating at weddings is a discretionary duty).

outside of court facilities.[20] These principles hold true even if a judge's decision not to conduct same-sex marriages reflects the judge's sincerely-held religious beliefs.[21]

Because performing marriages is a discretionary function, an Arizona judge may choose to perform no marriages.[22] An Arizona judge may also choose to perform marriages exclusively for family and friends without violating judicial conduct rules because the judge's practice is unrelated to the celebrants' sexual orientation.[23] If judges opt to perform marriages only for friends and relatives, however, they cannot ethically refuse to perform same-sex marriages for friends and relatives.[24] To do so would violate Arizona Rule of Judicial Conduct 2.3(B), which prohibits judges who are performing judicial duties from manifesting bias or prejudice based on sexual orientation.[25]

The Nebraska Judicial Ethics Committee reached essentially the same conclusion. In Opinion 15-1, the Nebraska Committee held that judges may not refuse to perform same-sex marriages notwithstanding their personal or sincerely-held religious beliefs that marriage is limited to the union of one man and one woman.[26] Nor may a judge refuse to perform a same-sex wedding if he or she refers the couple to a judge who is willing to perform same-sex marriages because the refusal to perform the ceremony manifests bias or prejudice based on the couple's sexual orientation notwithstanding the referral.[27] A judge may choose to avoid such personal or religious conflicts by refusing to perform marriages altogether.[28] Judges may also choose to perform marriages exclusively for close friends and relatives, but if they do so, they may not refuse to perform same-sex marriages for close friends and relatives.[29]

---

20. Ariz. Sup. Ct., Judicial Ethics Advisory Comm. Op. 15-01, 2015 WL 1530659, at *1 (2015).
21. *Id.*
22. *Id.*
23. *Id.* at *2.
24. *Id.* (citing Rule 2.3(B)).
25. *Id.*
26. Neb. Judicial Ethics Comm. Op. 15-1, at 2 (2015), *available at* https://supremecourt.nebraska.gov/sites/default/ files/ethics-opinions/Judicial/15-1_0.pdf.
27. *Id.*
28. *Id.*
29. *Id.*

Analysis

The public is entitled to expect that judges will perform their activities and duties fairly, impartially, and free from bias and prejudice.[30] Further, while actual impartiality is necessary, it is not sufficient; the public must also *perceive* judges to be impartial.[31]

If state law authorizes or obligates a judge to perform marriages, a judge's refusal to perform same-sex marriages while agreeing to perform marriages for opposite-sex couples is improper under Rules 1.1, 2.2, 2.3(A), and 2.3(B) Model Code. This conclusion would have been true in any state that recognized same-sex marriages before the Supreme Court decided *Obergefell v. Hodges*,[32] but it is broadly correct now. In *Obergefell*, the Supreme Court held that the Fourteenth Amendment to the U.S. Constitution prohibits states from refusing to license marriages between individuals of the same sex. As the Court explained, the U.S. Constitution "does not permit the State to bar same-sex couples from marriage on the same terms as accorded to couples of the opposite sex."[33] The Court further determined that "there is no lawful basis for a State to refuse to recognize a lawful same-sex marriage performed in another State on the ground of its same-sex character."[34]

---

30. *See generally* Liteky v. United States, 510 U.S. 540, 558 (1994) (Kennedy, J., concurring) (noting that judicial impartiality in both fact and appearance is "one of the very objects of law"); Alexander v. Primerica Holdings, 10 F.3d 155, 162 (3d Cir. 1993) (noting the importance of "'the public's confidence in the judiciary, which may be irreparably harmed if a case is allowed to proceed before a judge who appears to be tainted'") (citations omitted); United States v. CBS, 497 F.2d 107, 109 (5th Cir. 1974) (observing that "the protection of the integrity and dignity of the judicial process from any hint or appearance of bias is the palladium of our judicial system").

31. *See* Caperton v. A.T. Massey Coal Co., 556 U.S. 868, 888–89 (2009).

32. 135 S. Ct. 2584 (2015).

33. *Id.* at 2607; *see also id.* at 2604–2605 (stating that "the right to marry is a fundamental right inherent in the liberty of the person, and under the Due Process and Equal Protection Clauses of the Fourteenth Amendment couples of the same-sex may not be deprived of that right and that liberty").

34. *Id.* at 2607–2608. We recognize that a judge's refusal to perform a same-sex marriage may be based on the judge's sincerely-held beliefs regarding the concept of marriage. As the Supreme Court noted in *Obergefell*, "[m]any who deem same-sex marriage to be wrong reach that conclusion based on decent and honorable religious or philosophical principles, and neither they nor their beliefs are disparaged here." *Id.* at 2602. We also recognize, as the Supreme Court observed in *Masterpiece Cakeshop, Ltd. v. Colorado Civil Rights Comm'n*, 138 S. Ct. 1719 (2018), that the First Amendment ensures that people receive proper protection as

Model Rule 1.1 obligates judges to comply with the law. *Obergefell* makes clear that the U.S. Constitution prohibits state officials from engaging in discrimination and bias toward gays and lesbians in decisions related to same-sex marriage; in short, the decision establishes law with which judges must comply. Model Rule 2.2 requires judges to "uphold and apply [this] law," and further directs that judges "perform all duties of judicial office fairly and impartially."[35] As noted earlier, the term "impartiality" as used in this context means "the absence of bias or prejudice in favor of, or against, particular parties or classes of parties."[36]

Furthermore, Model Rule 2.3(A) specifically requires judges to perform their duties free from bias and prejudice. Model Rule 2.3(B) prohibits a judge who is performing judicial duties from manifesting bias or prejudice based on sex, gender, sexual orientation, or marital status. Indeed, we are aware of no state judicial ethics opinion concluding that similar judicial code provisions permit judges who perform marriage ceremonies for opposite sex couples to refuse to perform marriage ceremonies for same-sex couples.

A judge may choose to perform no marriages, or to perform marriages exclusively for family and friends. If judges opt to perform marriages only for friends and relatives, however, they cannot refuse to perform same-sex marriages for friends and relatives. Again, to refuse to perform same-sex marriages for friends and relatives while performing marriages of opposite-sex friends and relatives would violate Model Rules 2.2, 2.3(A), and 2.3(B). The fact that the judge's conduct affects a smaller group of people—that is, friends and family versus the public at large—does not change the judge's ethical obligations.

Our conclusions are reinforced by the Oregon Supreme Court's decision in *In re Day*.[37] The respondent in that case, Judge Vance Day,

they seek to live according to the principles of their religious faith. *Id.* at 1727. *Masterpiece Cakeshop* also underscored the fundamental importance of impartiality on the part of all officials vested by the state with adjudicative authority. *Id.* at 1721 (noting that biased comments and differential treatment on the part of a state agency "cast doubt on the fairness and impartiality of the Commission's adjudication"). But as noted earlier and reiterated here, this opinion addresses the obligations of judicial officers under the Model Code.

35. MODEL CODE R. 2.2, *supra* note 1.
36. *Id.* at Terminology.
37. 413 P.3d 907 (Or. 2018), *cert. denied*, 139 S. Ct. 324 (2018); *see also In re Neely*, 390 P.3d 728, 753 (Wyo. 2017) ("Judge Neely must perform her judicial

was appointed to the Oregon trial court bench in 2011 and re-elected in 2012. He made himself available to solemnize marriages upon becoming a judge in 2011.

After an Oregon federal judge invalidated Oregon's constitutional ban on same-sex marriage in 2014, Day's judicial assistant and clerk asked him about possibly performing weddings going forward given Day's religious belief that marriage should be confined to a man and a woman.[38] Judge Day "instructed [his clerk and judicial assistant] that, when his chambers received any marriage request, [they] should obtain" personal gender information available in the Oregon Judicial Information Network (OJIN)—which they had never done before—to try to determine whether the request involved a same-sex couple.[39] If it did, they were to inform the couple that the judge was not available on the desired date or otherwise notify him, so that he could decide how to proceed.[40] If the request came from an opposite-sex couple, however, his judicial assistant and clerk were to schedule the wedding.[41] On one occasion Day's judicial assistant checked OJIN and determined that the requesters might be a same-sex couple. Day had a genuine scheduling conflict, so the judicial assistant truthfully told the couple that the judge was unavailable. Day stopped performing marriages soon thereafter.

The Oregon Commission on Judicial Fitness and Disability charged Day with violating Rule 3.3(B) of the Oregon Code of Judicial Conduct, which provides: "A judge shall not, in the performance of judicial duties, by words or conduct, manifest bias or prejudice . . . against parties, witnesses, lawyers, or others based on attributes including but not limited to, sex, gender identity, race, national origin, ethnicity, religion, sexual orientation, marital status, disability, age, socioeconomic status, or political affiliation and shall not permit court staff,

---

functions, including performing marriages, with impartiality. She must either commit to performing marriages regardless of the couple's sexual orientation, or cease performing all marriage ceremonies. This does not mean . . . that no judge can now turn down any request to perform a marriage. What it means is that no judge can turn down a request to perform a marriage for reasons that undermine the integrity of the judiciary by demonstrating a lack of independence and impartiality."), *cert. denied*, 138 S. Ct. 639 (2018).

38. *In re Day*, 413 P.3d at 921, 949.
39. *Id.* at 921–22, 949.
40. *Id.* at 922, 949.
41. *Id.*

court officials, or others subject to the judge's direction and control to do so."[42] The *In re Day* court easily concluded that the act of solemnizing marriages, once a judge has chosen to do so, constitutes a judicial duty under Oregon Rule 3.3(B).[43] That led the court to the question of whether Day had manifested bias or prejudice against same-sex couples. Day argued that he had not done so because he never actually refused to marry any same-sex couple as a result of his short-lived screening process.[44] According to Day, Oregon Rule 3.3(B) could not authorize punishment "for discrimination that did not occur against unknown parties."[45]

The *In re Day* court reasoned that to "manifest" bias or prejudice, "the act in question must be undertaken such that it is obvious to others" or "must be capable of perception."[46] To be sure, Day's screening process was not displayed or made known in a manner that was capable of perception by anyone outside his chambers. But that factor did not resolve the issue because his "chosen course of action—motivated by his intention to marry only opposite-sex couples—was evident to his staff."[47] His instructions to his staff in implementing his plan to avoid marrying same-sex couples "indisputably communicated to his staff his intention to treat same-sex couples who requested a marriage officiant differently from opposite-sex couples."[48] Furthermore, he instructed his staff to implement "that differential treatment, which included providing inaccurate information to same-sex couples. Those actions 'manifest[ed]' prejudice in the performance of judicial duties, within the meaning of [Oregon] Rule 3.3(B)."[49]

Next, Day contended that because no same-sex couple was denied the opportunity to marry by virtue of his screening process, he did not discriminate or manifest prejudice "against" any such couple as required for a violation of Oregon Rule 3.3(B).[50] While it was true that he never actually refused to marry a same-sex couple, the *In re Day*

---

42. *Id.* at 950 (quoting OREGON CODE OF JUDICIAL CONDUCT R. 3.3(B) (2013)).
43. *Id.*
44. *Id.* at 951.
45. *Id.*
46. *Id.*
47. *Id.* at 952.
48. *Id.*
49. *Id.*
50. *Id.*

court nevertheless concluded that Day's conduct manifested prejudice against others within the meaning of the rule.

We reiterate that, in prohibiting a judge from manifesting prejudice against court participants or others based on personal attributes, [Oregon] Rule 3.3(B) seeks to prevent judicial actions that impair the fairness of a proceeding or prompt an unfavorable view of the judiciary. Most commonly, problematic conduct likely would involve a judge's overt and prejudicial treatment of a particular person involved in a proceeding before the court—such as a litigant, juror, witness, or lawyer. . . . However, a judge could manifest prejudice against others based on personal attributes in a more general way that still could affect perceptions of fairness or prompt an unfavorable view of the judiciary. . . . Given the fundamental objective of [Oregon] Rule 3.3(B)—ensuring the public's trust in an impartial and fair judiciary—we conclude that that rule is not limited to a manifestation of prejudice against an identified, particular person. Rather, it may encompass an expression of bias against an identifiable group, based on personal characteristics, in the performance of judicial duties.[51]

Day crafted a screening process that was intended to ensure that he married only opposite-sex couples. The screening process demonstrated to his staff that, in exercising his judicial duty to solemnize marriages, he would not treat all couples fairly. That conduct, in turn, manifested prejudice against same-sex couples based on their sexual orientation in violation of Oregon Rule 3.3(B).[52]

Conclusion

A judge for whom performing marriages is either a mandatory part of his or her official duties or an optional exercise of judicial

---

51. *Id.* at 952–53 (citations omitted).

52. *Id.* at 953. Although the Court found that Day violated Rule 3.3(B), it did not consider this violation in calculating the three-year suspension it imposed, explaining that "[i]n light of the other, notably serious misconduct that the commission has proved by clear and convincing evidence, we conclude that—whether respondent's constitutional challenges are meritorious or not—our ultimate conclusion to impose a lengthy, three-year suspension remains the same." *Id.* at 954.

authority violates the Model Code of Judicial Conduct by refusing to perform marriages for same-sex couples while agreeing to perform marriages of opposite-sex couples. In a jurisdiction where a judge is not obligated to perform marriages, the judge may decline to perform all marriages for members of the public. A judge who chooses not to perform any marriages for the public may still perform marriages for family and friends, so long as the judge does not discriminate between same-sex and opposite-sex couples when performing marriages for family and friends.

Formal Opinion 488
September 5, 2019
Judges' Social or Close Personal Relationships with Lawyers or Parties as Grounds for Disqualification or Disclosure

Rule 2.11 of the Model Code of Judicial Conduct identifies situations in which judges must disqualify themselves in proceedings because their impartiality might reasonably be questioned—including cases implicating some familial and personal relationships—but it is silent with respect to obligations imposed by other relationships. This opinion identifies three categories of relationships between judges and lawyers or parties to assist judges in evaluating ethical obligations those relationships may create under Rule 2.11: (1) acquaintanceships; (2) friendships; and (3) close personal relationships. In short, judges need not disqualify themselves if a lawyer or party is an acquaintance, nor must they disclose acquaintanceships to the other lawyers or parties. Whether judges must disqualify themselves when a party or lawyer is a friend or shares a close personal relationship with the judge or should instead take the lesser step of disclosing the friendship or close personal relationship to the other lawyers and parties, depends on the circumstances. Judges' disqualification in any of these situations may be waived in accordance and compliance with Rule 2.11(C) of the Model Code.[1]

I. Introduction

The Committee has been asked to address judges' obligation to disqualify[2] themselves in proceedings in which they have social or close personal relationships with the lawyers or parties other than a spousal, domestic partner, or other close family relationship. Rule 2.11 of the Model Code of Judicial Conduct ("Model Code") lists situations

---

1. This opinion is based on the MODEL CODE OF JUDICIAL CONDUCT as amended by the House of Delegates through February 2019. Individual jurisdictions' court rules, laws, opinions, and rules of professional conduct control. The Committee expresses no opinion on the applicable law or constitutional interpretation in a particular jurisdiction.

2. The terms "recuse" and "disqualify" are often used interchangeably in judicial ethics. *See* MODEL CODE OF JUDICIAL CONDUCT R. 2.11 cmt. 1 (2011) [hereinafter MODEL CODE] (noting the varying usage between jurisdictions). We have chosen to use "disqualify" because that is the term used in the Model Code of Judicial Conduct.

in which judges must disqualify themselves in proceedings because their impartiality might reasonably be questioned—including cases implicating some specific family and personal relationships—but the rule provides no guidance with respect to the types of relationships addressed in this opinion.[3]

Public confidence in the administration of justice demands that judges perform their duties impartially, and free from bias and prejudice. Furthermore, while actual impartiality is necessary, the public must also perceive judges to be impartial. The Model Code therefore requires judges to avoid even the appearance of impropriety in performing their duties.[4] As part of this obligation, judges must consider the actual and perceived effects of their relationships with lawyers and parties who appear before them on the other participants in proceedings.[5] If a judge's relationship with a lawyer or party would cause the judge's impartiality to reasonably be questioned, the judge must disqualify himself or herself from the proceeding.[6] Whether a judge's relationship with a lawyer or party may cause the judge's impartiality to reasonably be questioned and thus require disqualification is (a) evaluated against an objective reasonable person standard;[7] and (b) depends on the facts of the case.[8] Judges are presumed to be impartial.[9] Hence, judicial disqualification is the exception rather than the rule.

---

3. *See* MODEL CODE R. 2.11(A) (listing relationships where a judge's impartiality might reasonable be questioned, including where (1) the judge has "a personal bias or prejudice" toward a lawyer or party; (2) the judge's spouse, domestic partner, or a person within the third degree of relationship to the judge or the judge's spouse or domestic partner is a party or a lawyer in the proceeding; or (3) such person has more than a de minimis interest in the matter or is likely to be a material witness).

4. MODEL CODE R. 1.2.

5. *See* MODEL CODE R. 2.4(B) (stating that a judge shall not permit family or social interests or relationships to influence the judge's judicial conduct or judgment).

6. MODEL CODE R. 2.11(A).

7. Mondy v. Magnolia Advanced Materials, Inc., 815 S.E.2d 70, 75 (Ga. 2018); State v. Payne, 488 S.W.3d 161, 166 (Mo. Ct. App. 2016); Thompson v. Millard Pub. Sch. Dist. No. 17, 921 N.W.2d 589, 594 (Neb. 2019).

8. N.Y. Advisory Comm. on Judicial Ethics Op. 11-125, 2011 WL 8333125, at *1 (2011) [hereinafter N.Y. Jud. Adv. Op. 11-125].

9. Isom v. State, 563 S.W.3d 533, 546 (Ark. 2018); L.G. v. S.L., 88 N.E.3d 1069, 1073 (Ind. 2018); State v. Nixon, 254 So.3d 1228, 1235 (La. Ct. App. 2018); *Thompson*, 921 N.W.2d at 594.

Judges are ordinarily in the best position to assess whether their impartiality might reasonably be questioned when lawyers or parties with whom they have relationships outside of those identified in Rule 2.11(A) appear before them.[10] After all, relationships vary widely and are unique to the individuals involved. Furthermore, a variety of factors may affect judges' decisions whether to disqualify themselves in proceedings. For example, in smaller communities and relatively sparsely-populated judicial districts, judges may have social and personal contacts with lawyers and parties that are unavoidable. In that circumstance, too strict a disqualification standard would be impractical to enforce and would potentially disrupt the administration of justice. In other situations, the relationship between the judge and a party or lawyer may have changed over time or may have ended sufficiently far in the past that it is not a current concern when viewed objectively. Finally, judges must avoid disqualifying themselves too quickly or too often lest litigants be encouraged to use disqualification motions as a means of judge-shopping, or other judges in the same court or judicial circuit or district become overburdened.

Recognizing that relationships vary widely, potentially change over time, and are unique to the people involved, this opinion provides general guidance to judges who must determine whether their relationships with lawyers or parties require their disqualification from proceedings, whether the lesser remedy of disclosing the relationship to the other parties and lawyers involved in the proceedings is initially sufficient, or whether neither disqualification nor disclosure is required. This opinion identifies three categories of relationships between judges and lawyers or parties to assist judges in determining what, if any, ethical obligations Rule 2.11 imposes: (1) acquaintanceships; (2) friendships;[11] and (3) close personal relationships. Judges need not disqualify

---

10. N.Y. Jud. Adv. Op. 11-125, *supra* note 8, at *2.

11. Social media, which is simply a form of communication, uses terminology that is distinct from that used in this opinion. Interaction on social media does not itself indicate the type of relationships participants have with one another either generally or for purposes of this opinion. For example, Facebook uses the term "friend," but that is simply a title employed in that context. A judge could have Facebook "friends" or other social media contacts who are acquaintances, friends, or in some sort of close personal relationship with the judge. The proper characterization of a person's relationship with a judge depends on the definitions and examples used in this opinion.

themselves in proceedings in which they are acquainted with a lawyer or party. Whether judges must disqualify themselves when they are friends with a party or lawyer or share a close personal relationship with a lawyer or party or should instead disclose the friendship or close personal relationship to the other lawyers and parties, depends on the nature of the friendship or close personal relationship in question. The ultimate decision of whether to disqualify is committed to the judge's sound discretion.

II. Analysis

Rule 2.11(A) of the Model Code provides that judges must disqualify themselves in proceedings in which their impartiality might reasonably be questioned and identifies related situations. Perhaps most obviously, under Rule 2.11(A)(1), judges must disqualify themselves when they have a personal bias or prejudice concerning a party or a party's lawyer, or personal knowledge of facts that are in dispute in the proceeding. The parties may not waive a judge's disqualification based on personal bias or prejudice.[12]

Beyond matters in which the judge's alleged or perceived personal bias or prejudice is at issue, Rule 2.11(A) identifies situations in which a judge's personal relationships may call into question the judge's impartiality. Under Rule 2.11(A)(2), these include proceedings in which the judge knows that the judge, the judge's spouse or domestic partner, or a person within the third degree of relationship to either of them, or the spouse or domestic partner of such a person (a) is a party to the proceeding, or is a party's officer, director, general partner, or managing member; (b) is acting as a lawyer in the proceeding; (c) has more than a de minimis interest that could be affected by the proceeding; or (d) is likely to be a material witness in the proceeding. Under Rule 2.11(A)(4), a judge may further be required to disqualify himself or herself if a party, the party's lawyer, or that lawyer's law firm has made aggregate contributions to the judge's election or retention campaign within a specified number of years that exceed a specified amount or an amount that is reasonable and appropriate for an individual or entity. But, while Rule 2.11(A) mandates judges' disqualification in these situations, Rule 2.11(C) provides that a judge may disclose on the record the basis of the judge's disqualification

---

12. MODEL CODE R. 2.11(C).

and may ask the parties and their lawyers whether they waive disqualification. If the parties and lawyers agree that the judge should not be disqualified, the judge may participate in the proceeding.[13]

Apart from the personal relationships identified in Rule 2.11(A), a judge may have relationships with other categories of people that, depending on the facts, might reasonably call into question the judge's impartiality. These include acquaintances, friends, and people with whom the judge shares a close personal relationship.

A. Acquaintances

A judge and lawyer should be considered acquaintances when their interactions outside of court are coincidental or relatively superficial, such as being members of the same place of worship, professional or civic organization, or the like.[14] For example, the judge and the lawyer might both attend bar association or other professional meetings; they may have represented co-parties in litigation before the judge ascended to the bench; they may meet each other at school or other events involving their children or spouses; they may see each other when socializing with mutual friends; they may belong to the same country club or gym; they may patronize the same businesses and periodically encounter one another there; they may live in the same area or neighborhood and run into one another at neighborhood or area events, or at homeowners' meetings; or they might attend the same religious services. Generally, neither the judge nor the lawyer seeks contact with the other, but they greet each other amicably and are cordial when their lives intersect.[15]

A judge and party should be considered acquaintances in the same circumstances in which a judge and lawyer would be so characterized. Additionally, a judge and party may be characterized as acquaintances where the party owns or operates a business that the judge patronizes on the same terms as any other person.

---

13. Disqualification may not be waived where the judge harbors a personal bias or prejudice toward a party or a party's lawyer. *See* MODEL CODE R. 2.11(A)(1) & (C).

14. N.Y. Jud. Adv. Op. 11-125, *supra* note 8, at *2.

15. *Id.*

Evaluated from the standpoint of a reasonable person fully informed of the facts,[16] a judge's acquaintance with a lawyer or party, standing alone, is not a reasonable basis for questioning the judge's impartiality.[17] A judge therefore has no obligation to disclose his or her acquaintance with a lawyer or party to other lawyers or parties in a proceeding. A judge may, of course, disclose the acquaintanceship if the judge so chooses.

B. Friendships

In contrast to simply being acquainted, a judge and a party or lawyer may be friends. "Friendship" implies a degree of affinity greater than being acquainted with a person; indeed, the term connotes some degree of mutual affection. Yet, not all friendships are the same; some may be professional, while others may be social. Some friends are closer than others. For example, a judge and lawyer who once practiced law together may periodically meet for a meal when their busy schedules permit, or, if they live in different cities, try to meet when one is in the other's hometown. Or, a judge and lawyer who were law school classmates or were colleagues years before may stay in touch through occasional calls or correspondence, but not regularly see one another. On the other hand, a judge and lawyer may exchange gifts at holidays and special occasions; regularly socialize together; regularly communicate and coordinate activities because their children are close friends and routinely spend time at each other's homes; vacation together with their families; share a mentor-protégé relationship developed while colleagues before the judge was appointed or elected to the bench; share confidences and intimate details of their lives; or, for various reasons, be so close as to consider the other an extended family member.

Certainly, not all friendships require judges' disqualification,[18] as the Seventh Circuit explained over thirty years ago:

---

16. *See* State v. Mouelle, 922 N.W.2d 706, 713 (Minn. 2019) ("In deciding whether disqualification is required, the relevant question is 'whether a reasonable examiner, with full knowledge of the facts and circumstances, would question the judge's impartiality.'" (quoting *In re* Jacobs, 802 N.W.2d 748, 753 (Minn. 2011)).

17. N.Y. Jud. Adv. Op. 11-125, *supra* note 8, 2011 WL 8333125, at *2; Va. Judicial Ethics Advisory Comm. Op. 01-08, 2001 WL 36352802, at *1, *2 (2001).

18. *See, e.g., In re* Complaint of Judicial Misconduct, 816 F.3d 1266, 1268 (9th Cir. 2016) (stating that "friendship between a judge and a lawyer, or other partici-

In today's legal culture friendships among judges and lawyers are common. They are more than common; they are desirable. A judge need not cut himself off from the rest of the legal community. Social as well as official communications among judges and lawyers may improve the quality of legal decisions. Social interactions also make service on the bench, quite isolated as a rule, more tolerable to judges. Many well-qualified people would hesitate to become judges if they knew that wearing the robe meant either discharging one's friends or risking disqualification in substantial numbers of cases. Many courts therefore have held that a judge need not disqualify himself just because a friend—even a close friend—appears as a lawyer.[19]

Judicial ethics authorities agree that judges need not disqualify themselves in many cases in which a party or lawyer is a friend.[20]

There may be situations, however, in which the judge's friendship with a lawyer or party is so tight that the judge's impartiality might reasonably be questioned. Whether a friendship between a judge and a lawyer or party reaches that point and consequently requires the

---

pant in a trial, without more, does not require recusal"); Schupper v. People, 157 P.3d 516, 520 (Colo. 2007) (reasoning that friendship between a judge and a lawyer is not a per se basis for disqualification; rather, a reviewing court should "look for those situations where the friendship is so close or unusual that a question of partiality might reasonably be raised"); In re Disqualification of Park, 28 N.E.3d 56, 58 (Ohio 2014) ("[T]he existence of a friendship between a judge and an attorney appearing before her, without more, does not automatically mandate the judge's disqualification . . . ."); In re Disqualification of Lynch, 985 N.E.2d 491, 493 (Ohio 2012) ("The reasonable person would conclude that the oaths and obligations of a judge are not so meaningless as to be overcome merely by friendship with a party's counsel."); State v. Cannon, 254 S.W.3d 287, 308 (Tenn. 2008) ("The mere existence of a friendship between a judge and an attorney is not sufficient, standing alone, to mandate recusal.").

19. United States v. Murphy, 768 F.2d 1518, 1537 (7th Cir. 1985).

20. U.S. Judicial Conf., Comm. on Codes of Conduct Advisory Op. No. 11, 2009 WL 8484525, at *1 (2009); Ariz. Supreme Ct., Judicial Ethics Advisory Comm. Op. 90-8, 1990 WL 709830, at *1 (1990) [hereinafter Ariz. Jud. Adv. Op. No. 11]; N.Y. Jud. Adv. Op. 11-125, *supra* note 8, 2011 WL 8333125, at *2. *But see* Fla. Supreme Ct., Judicial Ethics Advisory Comm. Op. No. 2012-37, 2012 WL 663576, at *1 (2012) (stating that a judge "must recuse from any cases in which the judge's [close personal] friend appears as a party, witness or representative" of the bank where the friend was employed).

judge's disqualification in the proceeding is essentially a question of degree.[21] The answer depends on the facts of the case.[22]

A judge should disclose to the other lawyers and parties in the proceeding information about a friendship with a lawyer or party "that the judge believes the parties or their lawyers might reasonably consider relevant to a possible motion for disqualification, even if the judge believes there is no basis for disqualification."[23] If, after disclosure, a party objects to the judge's participation in the proceeding, the judge has the discretion to either continue to preside over the proceeding or to disqualify himself or herself. The judge should put the reasons for the judge's decision to remain on the case or to disqualify himself or herself on the record.

C. Close Personal Relationships

A judge may have a personal relationship with a lawyer or party that goes beyond or is different from common concepts of friendship, but which does not implicate Rule 2.11(A)(2). For example, the judge may be romantically involved with a lawyer or party, the judge may desire a romantic relationship with a lawyer or party or be actively pursuing one, the judge and a lawyer or party may be divorced but remain amicable, the judge and a lawyer or party may be divorced but communicate frequently and see one another regularly because they share custody of children, or a judge might be the godparent of a lawyer's or party's child or vice versa.

---

21. *See Schupper*, 157 P.3d at 520 (explaining that friendship between a judge and a lawyer is not an automatic basis for disqualification; rather, a reviewing court should "look for those situations where the friendship is so close or unusual that a question of partiality might reasonably be raised"); Ariz. Jud. Adv. Op. No. 11, *supra* note 20, at *1 (suggesting that in weighing disqualification where a lawyer who is a friend appears in the judge's court, the judge should consider as one factor "the closeness of the friendship"); CHARLES G. GEYH ET AL., JUDICIAL CONDUCT AND ETHICS § 4.07[4], at 4-27 (5th ed. 2013) ("Whether disqualification is required when a friend appears as a party to a suit before a judge depends on how close the personal . . . relationship is between the judge and the party.").

22. N.Y. Jud. Adv. Op. 11-125, *supra* note 8, at *1.

23. *See* Model Code R. 2.11 cmt. [5] ("A judge should disclose on the record information that the judge believes the parties or their lawyers might reasonably consider relevant to a possible motion for disqualification, even if the judge believes there is no basis for disqualification.").

A judge must disqualify himself or herself when the judge has a romantic relationship with a lawyer or party in the proceeding, or desires or is pursuing such a relationship. As the New Mexico Supreme Court has observed, "the rationale for requiring recusal in cases involving family members also applies when a close or intimate relationship [between a judge and a lawyer appearing before the judge] exists because, under such circumstances, the judge's impartiality is questionable."[24] A judge should disclose other intimate or close personal relationships with a lawyer or party to the other lawyers and parties in the proceeding even if the judge believes that he or she can be impartial.[25] If, after disclosure, a party objects to the judge's participation in the proceeding, the judge has the discretion to either continue to preside over the proceeding or to disqualify himself or herself. The judge should put the reasons for the judge's decision to remain on the case or to disqualify himself or herself on the record.

D. Waiver

In accordance and compliance with Rule 2.11(C), a judge subject to disqualification based on a friendship or close personal relationship with a lawyer or party may disclose on the record the basis for the judge's disqualification and may ask the parties and their lawyers to consider whether to waive disqualification.[26] If the parties and lawyers agree that the judge should not be disqualified, the judge may participate in the proceeding. The agreement that the judge may participate in the proceeding must be put on the record of the proceeding.

III. Conclusion

Judges must decide whether to disqualify themselves in proceedings in which they have relationships with the lawyers or parties short of spousal, domestic partner, or other close familial relationships. This opinion identifies three categories of relationships between judges and lawyers or parties to assist judges in determining what, if any, ethical obligations those relationships create under Rule 2.11: (1) acquain-

---

24. *In re* Schwartz, 255 P.3d 299, 304 (N.M. 2011).

25. *See* Model Code R. 2.11 cmt. [5]. A judge who prefers to keep such a relationship private may disqualify himself or herself from the proceeding.

26. Disqualification may not be waived if the judge has a personal bias or prejudice concerning a party or a party's lawyer. MODEL CODE R. 2.11(C).

tances; (2) friendships; and (3) close personal relationships. In summary, judges need not disqualify themselves if a lawyer or party is an acquaintance, nor must they disclose acquaintanceships to the other lawyers or parties. Whether judges must disqualify themselves when a party or lawyer is a friend or shares a close personal relationship with

INDEX

A

Adjudicative responsibilities,
    Ex parte communications
        Rule 2.9(A)(3)
Administrative law judges,
    Applicability of Code to
        Application, footnote 1
Administrative duties,
    Bias or prejudice
        Rule 2.3(A)
    Competence, diligence and cooperation
        Rule 2.5(A)
Administrator,
        Rule 3.8(A)
    See "Fiduciary," defined
    Terminology
Appearance of impropriety,
    Preamble
    Canon 1
    Rule 1.2
    Gifts
        Rule 3.13 (Comment)
    Invidious discrimination
        Rule 3.6 (Comment)
    Test for
        Rule 1.2 (Comment)
Appellate jurisdiction or authority,
    Application III(B)
    Application IV(B)
    Rule 2.9 (Comment)
    Rule 3.7(A)(2)
    Rule 3.7A(6)(b)
    Rule 3.8(B)

D

"De minimis" interest,
> Disqualification
>> Rule 2.11(A)(2)(c)
> Defined
>> Terminology
> *See* "Economic interest" defined
>> Terminology

Delay,
>> Rule 2.5 (Comment)

Dignity,
> Of judicial office
>> Preamble

Director,
> Judge's spouse, domestic partner, parent, or child serving as
>> Rule 2.11 (Comment)
> Serving as
>> Rule 3.7(A)(6)
>> Rule 3.11(b)

Disciplinary action,
>> Scope

Disciplinary responsibilities,
>> Rule 2.15, Rule 2.16

Disclosure,
> Of campaign contributions
>> Rule 4.4(B)(3)

Disqualification,
> In general
>> Rule 2.11
> Acceptance and reporting of gifts, loans, bequests, benefits, or other things of value
>> Rule 3.3(B)(2)
> Extrajudicial activities
>> Rule 3.1(B)
> Financial, business, or remunerative activities
>> Rule 3.11(C)(2)
> Information obtained during settlement discussions
>> Rule 2.6 (Comment)
> Responsibility to decide
>> Rule 2.7

E

F

See "Independence," defined
 Terminology
Investments,
 Holding and managing
  Rule 3.11
Invidious discrimination,
 Membership in organization that practices
  Rule 3.6

J

Judicial duties,
 See Adjudicative responsibilities
 See Administrative duties
 See Disciplinary responsibilities
Judicial selection,
 Communicating with appointing authority
  Rule 4.3(A)
 Cooperating with appointing authorities and screening
  committees
  Rule 1.3 (Comment)
Jurors,
 Appearance of bias or prejudice to
  Rule 2.3 (Comment)
 Communication with
  Rule 2.8

K

"Knowingly," "knowledge," "known" or "knows,"
 Defined
  Terminology
 Disqualification
  Rule 2.11
 False or misleading statements
  Rule 4.1(A)(11)
 Judicial or lawyer misconduct
  Rule 2.15(A) & (B)
 Organization practicing invidious discrimination
  Rule 3.6(B)

S

Scholarships,
    Accepting,
        Rule 3.3(B)(6)
Settling pending matters,
        Rule 2.9(A)(4)
Sexual harassment,
        Rule 2.3 (Comment)
Social hospitality,
    Accepting
        Rule 3.13(B)(3)
Solicit funds or contributions
    See "Personally solicit" defined
        Terminology
    Directions to campaign committee
        Rule 4.4(B)(1) & (2)
    For educational, religious, charitable, fraternal, or civic
    organization
        Rule 3.7(A)(2)
    For political organization or candidate
        Rule 4.1(A)(4)
    Personally
        Rule 4.1(A)(8)
Speaking,
    At program of educational, religious, charitable, fraternal, or
    civic organization
        Rule 3.7(A)(4)
    Compensation for
        Rule 3.12 (Comment)
    On behalf of candidacy
        Rule 4.2(B)(2)
Special master,
    Applicability of Code to
        Application I(B)
    Appointment as
        Rule 2.13 (Comment)
Statements
    Campaign
        Rule 4.2(A)(3)